ADVANCE PRAISE

"*Doing Business in India* is an informative and enlightening piece about all things India. From tourists to entrepreneurs, readers will find value from this informative and easy-to-understand resource. Topics range from Indian geography, culture and religion to travel requirements and business developments and protocols. Every chapter is well-developed and written so that readers can walk away with a breadth of knowledge and feel prepared to embark on their business ventures in the rising economy of India."

Savitaraj Hiremath, Founder and CEO,
Tandav Film Entertainment Pvt Ltd,
well-known producer for Path-Breaking
Bollywood Cinema and winner of
National and International Awards

"This book offers a sincere and practical approach that will change the pre-set mind of any foreigner to rethink doing business in India. To run a business smoothly in India it is necessary to satisfy the cultural importance of every region. The authors have taken into account India's diversified conditions in respect of language, cuisine, costume, religion and customs.

"The authors incorporate understanding and insights into complex business situations in India, taking into consideration legal formalities, market opportunities, taxation and other government regulations. This book will surely inspire anyone to think positively about India and about doing business in India while working and travelling with peace of mind, safety and security."

Anuj Rawat, CEO, India Travel and Leisure

"I've been travelling to India since 2011 to teach life skills workshops and network with global entrepreneurs. The business opportunities in India are limitless! This is the book I wish I had from the beginning to better understand the business and personal culture and traditions of this amazing country."

Ann Webb, Founder, Ideal LifeVision
and Global LifeVision

"A nicely detailed book giving a broad picture of Indian routine and lifestyle. Several valuable points covering everything from the challenges Indians face every day to important business details provided for those willing to venture into Indian markets."

Gaurav Singh, Postbaccalaureate,
Business Administration and Management

"This book will inspire those who have ever wondered about doing business in India. The authors have provided a vast array of essential information that will educate entrepreneurs, organizations and individuals. More importantly, they have personally lived and worked in India to gain an in-depth understanding of how to successfully bring business cultures together."

Benson Massey, CEO, Abish Travels
and Co-founder, Lift Lives Today

"*Doing Business in India* is a fantastic and quick guide on India, its culture and regions, and things to keep in mind before doing business here. It reminded me of my school days using a 'kunji', a small book outlining key questions likely to come up in exams: if you mastered the book's content you were sure to pass. One can never know everything about a country (I still struggle with some regions in India with it being so diverse) but this book is surely a good starting point before you enter this wonderland and my favourite place on earth."

Shivani Lorai, Founder and CEO,
WeWorld Consultants LLP

Published by
LID Publishing Limited
The Record Hall, Studio 204,
16-16a Baldwins Gardens,
London EC1N 7RJ, UK

info@lidpublishing.com
www.lidpublishing.com

A member of:

www.businesspublishersroundtable.com

© Jamie Cid & Laurie Baum, 2019
© LID Publishing Limited, 2019

Printed in the Czech Republic by Finidr
ISBN: 978-1-912555-34-5

Cover and page design: Caroline Li

WORLD WISE

DOING BUSINESS IN *INDIA*

JAMIE CID & LAURIE BAUM

MADRID | MEXICO CITY | LONDON
NEW YORK | BUENOS AIRES
BOGOTA | SHANGHAI | NEW DELHI

CONTENTS

1   ACKNOWLEDGMENTS

6   *PART 1* – INTRODUCTION
     Who is This Book For?
     Topics Include
     Why Doing Business in India is a Good Idea

18   *PART 2* – THE COUNTRY
     Overview of India
     Geography
     Climate
     Population
     Language
     History of India
     Government and Politics

50   *PART 3* – CULTURE: SOCIETY, HIERARCHY
     AND RELIGION
     Culture and Society Overview
     Hierarchy in Society
     Religion
     Well-known Indians

76   *PART 4* – CULTURE: HOLIDAYS,
     CUISINE, ART AND MISCONCEPTIONS
     National Holidays and Festivals
     Indian Cuisine
     Art, Music, Dance, Bollywood
     Stereotypes and Misconceptions
     Indian Social Phenomena

120   *PART 5 –* TRAVEL, HEALTH AND SAFETY
      Before You Arrive
      Arriving in India
      Getting Around in India
      Healthcare in India
      Travel Insurance
      Safety
      Safety Especially for Women
      Emergency Contacts

144   *PART 6 –* TOP TRAVEL DESTINATIONS
      AND ATTRACTIONS
      North
      Northwest
      Northeast
      East
      South
      Southwest

156   *PART 7 –* BUSINESS ETIQUETTE AND PROTOCOL
      Business Hierarchies
      Greetings
      Decision-making Styles and Business Negotiations
      Characteristics of Employers
      Characteristics of Employees
      Food and Drink, Gifts and Entertainment
      International Relations

170   *PART 8 –* STARTING YOUR BUSINESS IN INDIA
      Market Entry Structures and Strategies
      Market Opportunities
      Business Wisdom
      Support for Business
      Legal and Regulatory Framework

Key Organizations/Bodies to Assist International Business
FDI Restrictions to Consider
Taxation and Government Incentives
Startup Tax Incentives
Managing Money

196   *PART 9 – THINGS TO CONSIDER WHEN*
      DOING BUSINESS IN INDIA
      Hiring and Building a Team
      Demonetization and Digital India
      Finding Customers in India
      Finding the Right Pricing
      Intellectual Property Risks and Strategies
      Strategy to Protect Your Ideas
      Corruption Awareness and The Bribery Act of 2010

214   *PART 10 – BUSINESS BY REGION*
      Doing Business in East India
      Doing Business in Northeast India
      Doing Business in West India
      Doing Business in North India
      Doing Business in South India

240   *PART 11 – CONCLUSION: THE EVER-CHANGING*
      DEVELOPMENT OF INDIA

244   *BIBLIOGRAPHY*

247   *ABOUT THE AUTHORS*

ACKNOWLEDGMENTS

After 15 years of travelling to India and spending the last four years living there, it was no surprise that this first book came to life as part of the 'World Wise Series'. India has been my home away from home and a school itself. I thank everyone who has been part of this journey for the last few years.

I thank my colleagues at Pearl Academy who inspired me and showed me what talented, passionate teachers and students of India are like when they love what they do. The students at Pearl allowed me to share my entrepreneurial journey and inspired me to teach and speak on entrepreneurship in Delhi and abroad. Thank you, team Pearl, and special thanks to Meha Jeyaswal, a teacher and head of the Media Department with a passion for inspiring students to be their best. Her support and belief in me make me feel truly blessed to have such a wonderful mentor and friend.

Thank you, Founders Institute and TieNY, for creating organizations that inspire, encourage and empower entrepreneurs in India and for giving me the opportunity to mentor Indian startup founders over the last five years.

Thanks to team SHEROES for their support as I explored a creative solution for the Indian market and for inviting me to be part of the conversation inspiring Indian female entrepreneurs.

Thank you team Mobihires, Sathish, Dencer, Sambu, Jessica, Ananth, Nikki, Arijit and Aakash.

To my co-workers at Ramco and Aricent, thank you for helping me to understand the minds of North and South Indian residents and their unique differences.

To my co-author Laurie Baum, for taking on the challenge of writing this introduction to business in India with me. I look forward to many more writing adventures. Thank you to WEF, Harbeen, Vinay and Yoon for making the connection.

Finally, thank you to my family – parents, siblings, niece, nephew and inner circle – for being the best support system a girl looking to make a difference can have. Through my most challenging times you have been there. That's all entrepreneurs need: honest feedback, friendly support and constant open ears.

Thank you to my guru Sathya Sai Baba – without him, I would not have landed in India in 2001 to explore its beauty, its people and the many opportunities it offers.

I hope this book inspires those who read it to take on the challenge of exploring India and understanding that, while it is a complex nation, it's a place ready for change and true growth, and it is a nation transforming right in front of our eyes.

Special acknowledgments to: Francisco, Magdalena, Liz, Francis, David, Maia, Ethan, Jackie, the Lee Family, Pushita, Danielle, Rishika, Bawa, the Sai Family and all those who have personally been part of my life in NY, NJ and Delhi.

In Gratitude
Jamie Cid

could write volumes thanking all those who have contributed to my learning experiences while working in India – perhaps someday I will, but until then I welcome the opportunity to recognize and thank a few. Thank you, Jamie Cid, for inviting me to share in this new and exciting adventure! To LID Publishing and your entire team for your guidance and for trusting us to bring India to life in your 'World Wise Series'.

To Ann Webb – if it weren't for you I may have never set foot on Indian soil. Thank you for teaching me how to dream bigger and to hold the vision for my wildest imagination, and for encouraging me to finally push the 'send' button on the email that changed my life.

To Vinay Rai, for extending my first invitation to come to India teaching underprivileged girls, which opened both my mind and many doors in ways I could have never imagined. Many thanks to you and Harbeen Arora for offering me my first job in India, from which I learned some of my most profound discoveries about India and about myself.

To Charu Acharya, for making sure my transition into living and working in India was met with ease and warmth. Your steady attention to detail and delightful presence made all the difference. To Yoon Cho – there's no doubt we could have easily had our own reality show about two foreigners from the US and South Korea learning to live and work in India! To Pravin Singh and Shiv Kumar – I didn't know a word of Hindi, and you didn't know a word of English. Communicating through charades and laughing until our sides ached was a daily occurrence. Not only did you do your job, but I knew you genuinely cared, and that's what makes you so special.

To my Rai University colleagues, thank you for your patience with me and for your example in teaching the youth of India with great passion. To all my students whom I affectionately call 'the generation of hope, courage and change', you inspire me. I came to India to teach, yet it was I who learned the most from you.

To the entire Women Economic Forum team – also known as the 'Dream Team' – I was inspired time and time again by your ingenuity and determination. Thank you for your willingness and patience to work with an American learning the ropes of Indian business culture. To Magdalena Sieradzka – how two girls from the US and Poland ended up in Delhi working with an office full of Indians still astounds me.

To Rachna Thakur, Gaurav Singh, Karan Hemnani, Yash Singh and Benson Massey, thank you for answering a million questions, for your candid expressions of life as it truly is and for welcoming me into your homes: most of all, thank you for your friendship. Thank you to my love posse of friends around the world for your ever-present encouragement – I felt your love and it made all the difference.

To Shubham Sharma, I have literally placed my life in your hands more than once. Thank you for your never-ending patience when I'd lost all of mine. You have become family, my protector, my navigator, my trusted business partner, and my calm when my heart is in a storm.

Special thanks to my family for your love and support, especially when you all thought I had completely lost my mind when I packed up two suitcases and moved to India.

To the people of India, you truly amaze and inspire me every day. You have taught me the most important things in life and have welcomed me warmly into your country, your hearts and your homes. It's been said before that it would take three lifetimes to understand Indian culture – I hold in gratitude those who took the time to teach me in this lifetime.

I was not born in India, but India was born in me.

Laurie Baum

PART 1

INTRODUCTION

WHO IS THIS BOOK FOR?

This book is designed as an introduction for individuals, entrepreneurs and small- to medium-sized enterprises as a general overview of the fundamentals of doing business in India. Included are some specifics of India's culture and values, as well as business practices and etiquette, along with insider tips to help create a successful business partnership. The information contained in this book will help provide a deeper understanding of India's business and personal relationships to minimize cross-cultural mishaps and misunderstandings.

This book has been written using the most up-to-date information available at the time of publication. Jamie Cid and Laurie Baum have used their personal experiences from working in India, information gleaned from interviews with both Indians and foreigners doing business in India, and additional resources and research to create this book.

TOPICS INCLUDE

- Why doing business in India is a good idea
- An introduction to India, its history, population, languages, politics, food, religions, national holidays, festivals and more
- An understanding of India's traditions and culture and their impact on daily life
- The many stereotypes and misconceptions about India
- Guidelines for adapting to and accepting cultural differences
- Indian business practices and etiquette
- Practical information and useful links
- Mistakes you wouldn't want to repeat: dos, don'ts and taboos

WHY DOING BUSINESS IN INDIA IS A GOOD IDEA

India is a country known for its rich cultural heritage, ancient architecture, vibrant colours, vast array of spices, exotic beauty and life full of diversity, extremes and contradictions.

India is also known as a rapidly rising global force with enormous economic opportunities and potential. India made waves on the international stage when it became the world's fastest growing economy in 2018 and continues an upward surge. The World Bank has forecast India's GDP to grow at 7.3% in the fiscal year 2018-19 and projects India's GDP to expand 7.5% in the following two years.[1]

India is currently ranked sixth in the top ten economies of the world. Predicted forecasts are favourable for India as it is projected to become the fifth-largest economy in the world by 2020, and by 2050 India's economy is projected to be the world's second-largest, behind only China.

India now makes up 15% of global growth fueled by several factors and demographic trends, including reforms, foreign investment and strong domestic demand.[2]

With an upswing in domestic consumption and investment – as well as the booming industries of power generation, tourism and hospitality, animation and food processing – these contributing factors all play an important role in driving India's strong economic growth.[3]

The ease of doing business in India is enhanced by the fact that English is an official language of India, giving further appeal to foreigners wanting to do business with this booming economy.

Before the age of European colonization, India accounted for roughly 25% of the world's manufactured goods. In the 13th century, India emerged with a great trading capacity and was able to achieve a state of economic dominance within the wider Indian Ocean world.

TOP 10 GLOBAL ECONOMIES

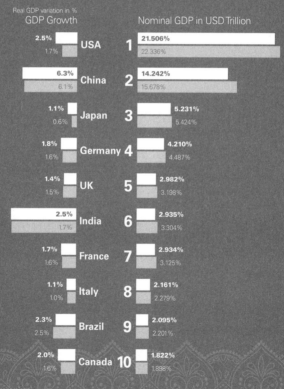

Real GDP variation in %
GDP Growth

Nominal GDP in USD Trillion

	GDP Growth		Rank		Nominal GDP in USD Trillion
USA	2.5% / 1.7%		1	21.506% / 22.336%	
China	6.3% / 6.1%		2	14.242% / 15.678%	
Japan	1.1% / 0.6%		3	5.231% / 5.424%	
Germany	1.8% / 1.6%		4	4.210% / 4.487%	
UK	1.4% / 1.5%		5	2.982% / 3.198%	
India	2.5% / 1.7%		6	2.935% / 3.304%	
France	1.7% / 1.6%		7	2.934% / 3.125%	
Italy	1.1% / 1.0%		8	2.161% / 2.279%	
Brazil	2.3% / 2.5%		9	2.095% / 2.201%	
Canada	2.0% / 1.6%		10	1.822% / 1.898%	

2019
2020

Source: Focus Economics

Owing to a number of government reforms, policies and various initiatives to increase confidence and boost growth, India has been improving its performance in a number of global rankings. India jumped 23 notches from the preceding year to rank 77th in the World Bank's 2018 *Ease of Doing Business* rankings. The report also recognized India as one of the top ten improvers for the second consecutive year. India became the only large country in 2018 to have achieved such a significant shift.

The research institute Oxford Economics remarkably predicts that between 2019 and 2035, the top ten fastest-growing cities by GDP in the world will all be found in India.[4]

- Surat, known for its diamond processing and growing IT sector, tops the list with a predicted average annual GDP growth rate of 9.2%.
- Agra is home to the Taj Mahal and comes in second with a predicted average annual GDP growth rate of 8.6%.
- Bengaluru, India's Silicon Valley, is expected to register a predicted average annual GDP growth rate of 8.5%.

Other fast-growing names include Hyderabad (8.47%), Nagpur (8.41%), Tiruppur (8.36%), Rajkot (8.33%), Tiruchirappalli (8.29%), Chennai (8.17%) and Vijay-awada (8.16%).

TOP 10 FASTEST GROWING GLOBAL CITIES

Rank	Growth (% y/y, 2019-35)	City	GDP 2018 ($ billion, constant 2018 prices)	GDP 2035 ($ billion, constant 2018 prices)
①	9.17	**Surat**	28.5	126.8
②	8.58	**Agra**	3.9	15.6
③	8.50	**Bengaluru**	70.8	283.3
④	8.47	**Hyderbad**	50.6	201.4
⑤	8.41	**Nagpur**	12.3	48.6
⑥	8.36	**Tiruppur**	4.3	17.0
⑦	8.33	**Rajkot**	6.8	26.7
⑧	8.29	**Tiruchirappalli**	4.9	19.0
⑨	8.17	**Chennai**	36.0	136.8
⑩	8.16	**Vijayawada**	5.6	21.3

Source: Oxford Economies

India is home to 1.34 billion people – with 18% of the world's population and predicted to overtake China as the world's most populous country by 2024. India's ever-growing middle-class average household disposable income will ignite explosive growth, producing considerable purchasing power. Couple that with the fact that India also holds the title for the world's largest youth population and India will be set to be the largest consumer market in the world.[5]

Approximately 60% of India's highest earners live in the country's ten largest cities with respect to GDP, and this is not expected to change in coming years. These high-end customers are a highly visible business market. These purchasing power cities are Mumbai, Delhi, Kolkata, Bengaluru, Chennai, Hyderabad, Pune, Ahmedabad, Surat and Vishakhapatnam.[6]

While income growth will continue to be the fastest in urban areas, rural areas are also predicted to grow. These traditionally poorer households are likely to enjoy an increased standard of living and rate of consumption as those living in urban areas.

Although India is a developing country, don't accept the notion that it is a poor country. India has immense wealth, but its population is also vast and many of them are poor. According to the 2018 'World Wealth Report', India was the fastest growing place globally in 2017 for High Net Worth Individuals, in terms of both population expansion and wealth growth. India is home to 20,730 multi-millionaires, the seventh-largest total in the world. India is also home to 119 resident billionaires, putting it in the top three countries globally, after the US and China.

India's emerging markets and improving infrastructure, combined with one of the world's largest pools of skilled, professional, fluent English-speaking workers, as well as a low-cost workforce, to provide an attractive landing place for many business opportunities.

India offers a unique combination of advantages with massive market growth and unlimited potential. Recent years have seen rapid growth in the country's economy, attracting foreign businesses, investors and multinational corporations. As more and more expatriates are drawn to doing business in India, its living and working environments have adapted to global standards.

INDIA'S STRENGTHS SPEAK FOR THEMSELVES:[7]

- A labour workforce over 400 million strong.
- A large and growing middle class, creating a steady increase in domestic demand.
- A deep English-language business environment.
- Cost competitiveness.
- World-class expertise in IT software and business process outsourcing.

In this era of globalization, doing business in India is a wise and progressive idea, but it will require different skills, patience, careful planning and perpetual flexibility.

As with any country, India is a product of its history. The important keys to unlocking your success in India will be in respecting and gaining perspective on India's social and business cultures, allowing you to glean and develop a solid understanding and awareness of the country and its extraordinary people.

Consumer spending in India is expected to triple by 2020. Indian consumer spending is projected to rise to $3.6 trillion in 2020, from $991 billion in 2010.

MAP OF INDIA

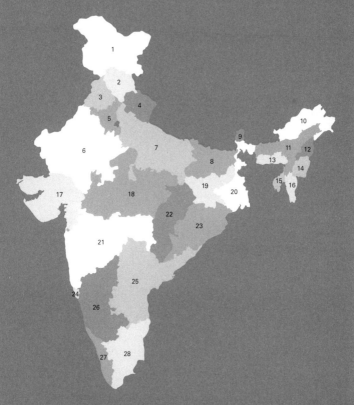

1	Jammu & Kashmir	**8**	Bihar	**15**	Tripura	**22**	Chhattisgarh
2	Himachal Pradesh	**9**	Sikkim	**16**	Mizoram	**23**	Odisha
3	Punjab	**10**	Arunachal Pradesh	**17**	Gujarat	**24**	Goa
4	Uttarakhand	**11**	Assam	**18**	Madhya Pradesh	**25**	Andhra Pradesh
5	Haryana	**12**	Nagaland	**19**	Jharkhand	**26**	Karnataka
6	Rajasthan	**13**	Meghalaya	**20**	West Bengal	**27**	Kerala
7	Uttar Pradesh	**14**	Manipur	**21**	Maharashtra	**28**	Tamil Nadu

PART 2

THE COUNTRY

OVERVIEW OF INDIA

India.

The name evokes images and thoughts that span the scope of the mind and imagination and stoke the mind with intrigue and curious notion. India has influenced nearly every aspect of Western living, including the food we eat, how we decorate our homes, what we wear, how we accessorize, how we exercise, how we relax, the way we worship, how we treat an illness, the movies we watch and the technology we use.

Viewed from afar, one's perceptions of India might be formed based on shocking headlines, its astounding population and unfathomable poverty, its place as a global technology leader, as well as its exotic art forms, exquisite beauty and ancient wisdom. While all of these things are a part of the reality of modern India, the true heartbeat of India is its people. Each region, religion, caste and community has its own culture, its own unique histories shaped by conviction and conquest, and its own expressions and expectations of daily life.

Indians live deeply committed to their traditions and have strong bonds to their family and society. Honour and respect play an unwavering role in daily life and in making life decisions. The people of India are intensely passionate about their culture and welcome the curiosity of foreigners. Indians are exceptionally hospitable and consider 'the guest is God'. There is nothing quite like a warm Indian welcome. Indians are some of the most ingenious, hard-working, fascinating and creative people in the world. Give a task to an Indian to figure out and it will often be done in quite unexpected ways, leaving you scratching your head in wonder and with an approving smile.

As you experience India up close, you will begin to understand its dualistic beliefs and behaviours. In many ways, India holds these contradictions simply because it contains within a single nation more diversity than most other countries, whether it's diversity of religion, caste, occupation, society or language. The struggle between the country's ancient ways of simplicity and modern materialism, extreme poverty co-existing with extreme wealth, sacred monuments carved with intricate designs, littered with posters advertising the latest technologies and beauty fads all capture the reality and the struggle of a country holding onto its past, while creating a new future.

In the face of the challenge of preserving 5,000-year-old customs and traditions, India is changing. However, in these times of unprecedented changes, in many ways India also remains the same. The chaos of the bustling streets, the pigments of colour, the smell of spices, the sounds of incessant horns honking – to the unfamiliar, these sights, sounds and smells are an overload to the senses that will challenge even the most experienced traveller.

India is both the beauty and the beast. Newcomer responses to India can be as diverse as the people and places they encounter. It is in the art of surrender that will bring a shift in observation and awareness to the many opportunities and allow you to embrace the essence of all India has to offer. With its brightest minds and a vibrant new generation dedicated to honouring its ancestors while pressing its beloved country forward, India is an ever-evolving force in the global conversation.

GEOGRAPHY

India is the seventh-largest country in the world and comprises most of the Indian subcontinent. India holds some of the most breathtaking and extraordinary natural geography. From the majestic Himalayan mountain peaks in the north to the exotic tropical beaches of the south, India's geography is vastly diverse. Within India, every possible geographical vista can be seen, from snow-laden mountains, green rolling hills, sparkling lakes and cascading waterfalls to dense tropical forests and sandy deserts.

The Indian peninsula is surrounded by the Bay of Bengal skirting around the shores to the east, the Arabian Sea to the west and the Indian Ocean to the south. India shares borders with Bangladesh and Myanmar to the east, China, Nepal and Bhutan to the northeast and Pakistan to the northwest. Off India's southeastern shore sits the island nation of Sri Lanka. Indigenous islanders inhabit the Indian Union Territories of the Andaman and Nicobar Islands, comprising roughly 300 islands in the Bay of Bengal, many of which are off limits to visitors.

The Ganges River flows from the western Himalayas and runs south and east through the plains of North India and into the Bay of Bengal. The Ganges (or 'Ganga') is one of the most sacred rivers to Hindus. It is also a lifeline to millions of Indians who live along its path and depend on it for their daily needs. Kangchenjunga is the highest mountain peak in India, ranking as the third-highest summit in the world with an elevation of 8,586 metres (28,169 feet). Kangchenjunga is located at the border of India and Nepal in the great Himalayas.

India is a federal union comprising 29 states and seven union territories. The states and union territories are further subdivided into districts and smaller administrative divisions. The capital of India is in the north, in the historical city of what is now called New Delhi.

CLIMATE

India's climate changes drastically with its immense geographical diversity. Tropical, subtropical, arid and alpine climate zones can all be found within this vast nation.

India typically falls under the category of a tropical monsoon climate, characterized by very high temperatures, heavy monsoon rains and cool, dry winters. India has four major seasons throughout the year:

- Summer: March-June
- Monsoon: July-September
- Post-monsoon/autumn: October-November
- Winter: December-February

Significant variations in different regions of the country present extremely important factors for consideration when planning any travel to India. Weather conditions in the extreme north are very different from those in the South. Monsoon seasons vary as well in different parts of the country.

Kerala in the southwest is tropical, with heavy rainfall and temperatures averaging 28-32°C /82-90°F. The southern tip of India enjoys temperatures similar to Hawaii nearly all year round. The rest of the country, however, has much less temperate weather.

The summer months of April to June see an average temperature of 32°C /90°F; however, the average temperatures in the deserts can reach 50°C /122°F or even higher. The Great Indian Desert covers much of Rajasthan and parts of Gujarat, along with the northern Himalayas, which block the cool winds from central Asia. As July and August approach, the heat and humidity are difficult for all who work or travel there. Monsoon season is in full swing with thunderstorms, sheets of rain and overflowing rivers, making daily life more challenging and sometimes dangerous.

From September to November, the monsoons subside in the west and shift to the east, drenching that region before slowly easing into winter. The winter season runs from December to February and is relatively dry and cool, with temperatures averaging 10-15°C /50-60°F. Southern regions are warmed by the surrounding waters of the Indian Ocean, the Bay of Bengal and the Arabian Sea.

In parts of the northeast, annual rainfall can be as high as 1,000 centimetres, or 394 inches, and in the north, parts of India see snow. Himachal Pradesh, Uttaranchal and Shimla are all known for their thriving ski resorts.

Generally, the best time to plan a visit to India for business or leisure is during the pleasant cool, dry season, between November and March. Outside of these months, travelling to most parts of India will greet you with sweltering temperatures and highly uncomfortable humid conditions.

Whether you're planning a business trip to India or want to enjoy some of the natural wonders, snow ski or lounge on the warm sandy beaches India has to offer, be sure to check the climate of the region at the time of year you wish to visit.

POPULATION

India is the second-most populated country in the world, after China, with an astounding population of 1,367,057,471 as of early 2019. This represents 17.74% of the total world population. India has many large cities that contribute to its massive population. There are 39 megacities that each have populations exceeding one million. Of these cities, five have populations that exceed ten million. India is also home to 388 cities with populations exceeding 100,000.[1,2]

India will become the world's youngest country by 2020 when the median age in India will become 29. The population in the 15-34 age group is expected to rise to 464 million in 2021.

MOST POPULATED INDIAN CITIES

❶ DELHI is home to the nation's capital with a rich history that dates back to the sixth century BC. Delhi and the National Capital Territory (NCT) is a large metropolitan area and includes the neighboring cities of Baghpat, Alwar, Sonepat, Gurgaon, Ghaziabad, Faridabad, Greater Noida, Noida and nearby towns. Delhi is an important commercial, transport and cultural hub as well as the political centre of India. It is the second-wealthiest city in India after Mumbai. *Population: 29,399,141.*

❷ MUMBAI *(Previously known as Bombay)* has one of the largest urban populations in the world. It is India's centre of entertainment, fashion, finance and commerce. Mumbai is the wealthiest city in India, with the highest numbers of millionaires and billionaires. *Population: 20,185,064.*

❸ KOLKATA *(Previously known as Calcutta)* is a city of major ports, commerce and manufacturing. Its vibrant traditions lie in the arts, including drama,

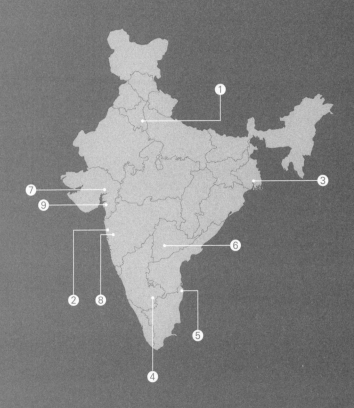

theatre, film and literature. *Population: 14,755,186.*

④ BENGALURU *(Previously known as Bangalore)* is the highly acclaimed information technology hub and the nation's leading IT exporter, earning the nickname 'Silicon Valley of India'. *Population: 11,882,666.*

❺ CHENNAI *(Previously known as Madras)* is South India's centre for education, economics and culture. Termed 'India's Health Capital', Chennai attracts 45% of medical/health tourists visiting India and 30-40% of domestic medical/health tourists.
Population: 10,711,243.

❻ HYDERABAD is known for its distinctive cuisine, with Biryani topping the list, as well as for its cultural history. Hyderabad is also home to Google's India headquarters.
Population: 9,741,397.

❼ AHMEDABAD has grown into an economic and industrial hub in India. Ahmedabad is also known for its textile mills and often referred to as the 'Manchester of the East'.
Population: 7,868,633.

❽ PUNE is a nationwide leader in the automotive and manufacturing industries. It is also known as the 'Oxford of the East' due to the presence of several well-known educational institutions.
Population: 6,451,618.

❾ SURAT was the world's fourth-fastest-growing city in 2016. It is known for producing textiles, especially silk and cotton, and is nicknamed the 'Diamond City of India' because of its highly qualified diamond cutting and polishing profession. Surat was selected as the country's first IT smart city.
Population: 6,873,756.

Major Indian cities are densely populated with humanity in all its forms. The traffic is beyond comprehension with a plethora of cars, buses, bikes, motorcycles, merchant carts, agricultural trucks and carts, rickshaws, street dwellers, cows and the occasional camel or elephant.

Horns are honking incessantly. While for most foreigners a horn honking is a sign of aggression, in India a horn honking is a sign of courtesy. It serves the purpose of saying, "Hey, I'm coming up to the side of you". There is no such thing as 'personal space' in India. Activities seen along the roadside span the scope of imagination, from mothers bathing their children to a barber setting up shop under a tree, to bustling street food stands, to exquisite clothing shops, a farmer herding his goats to luxury car dealerships. The chaos is mind-boggling, yet everyone seems to get to where they need to go. A major Indian city is evidence of life, in every form and function.

Though the urban population is huge, up to 70% of Indians still live in villages. However, migration to the cities is increasing due to loss of land or crops through flood or drought and the desire of many for better education and work opportunities. As India is on the path of development, there are still 70.6 million people living below the poverty line. Internationally, extreme poverty is defined as living on less than $1.90 a day. These people struggling against poverty usually live in slum areas connected to or within major cities. However, with progress – albeit slow progress – comes change. After decades of being at the very bottom, India was replaced in 2018 by Nigeria as the country with the world's highest number of people living in extreme poverty.

You might actually know a little Hindi if you have seen *The Jungle Book*. The names of the bear (Baloo), panther (Bagheera) and elephant (Hathi) are all taken directly from the Hindi words for these animals. Similarly, Shere Kahn comes from the Persian word 'Sher' (tiger) and the Arabic word 'Khan' (king). Hindi is heavily influenced by the Arabic and Persian languages. Rudyard Kipling wrote this book with inspiration from his childhood growing up in India.
– Hippie in Heels.

LANGUAGE

The Indian Constitution declares Hindi, written in Devanagari (देवनागरी) script, as the official language of India, with English as the secondary official language. The use of English comes from the British rule on the Indian subcontinent between 1858 and 1947. In addition to Hindi and English, the Constitution officially recognizes over 20 national languages; however, more than 2,000 languages and dialects have been identified. Linguistic researchers have found that two of the world's oldest written languages are from India, Sanskrit and Tamil. Sadly, Sanskrit has gradually fallen out of everyday use, but Tamil is still widely used in India.

While most countries in the world have one national language, India has a different language for each of its 29 states. The many languages spoken throughout the country are another reflection of the wide diversity of India. For this reason, it is common for Indians to know more than one language. Often, an Indian will know Hindi and English as well as the language of their mother state.

Most educated Indians speak three, four or five languages, or more.

Though India celebrates its linguistic diversity, this can also be problematic, even amongst its own people. Due to the hundreds of dialects used throughout the country, Indians themselves sometimes find it difficult to manage in parts of the country whose mother tongue is different from their own. The variations of intonation, the pitch, the way certain sounds linger or are stressed differ within regions.

India is the largest English-speaking country in the world. Modern Indians have invented a whole new language called *Hinglish*, a hybrid of Hindi and English spoken in many urban areas of India. The Hinglish language involves mixing Hindi and English within conversations, individual sentences and even words. It is not unusual to hear an Indian speaking a language you don't understand and suddenly hear an English word thrown into the mix of the conversation.

INDIA'S STATE/ TERRITORY LANGUAGES

Name of State	Major Language	Other Languages Spoken
Jammu And Kashmir	Kashmiri	Dogri And Hindi
Himachal Pradesh	Hindi	Punjabi And Nepali
Punjab	Punjabi	Hindi
Uttrakhand	Hindi	Urdu, Punjabi And Nepali
Haryana	Hindi	Punjabi And Urdu
Delhi	Hindi	Punjabi, Urdu And Bengali
Uttar Pradesh	Hindi	Urdu
Rajasthan	Hindi	Punjabi And Urdu
Madhya Pradesh	Hindi	Marathi And Urdu
Chhattisgarh	Hindi	Bengali And Oriya
Bihar	Hindi	Maithili And Urdu
Jharkhand	Hindi	Santali, Bengali And Urdu
West Bengal	Bengali	Hindi, Santali, Urdu, Nepali
Sikkim	Nepali	Hindi, Bengali
Assam	Assamese	Bengali, Hindi, Bodo And Nepali
Arunachal Pradesh	Bengali	Nepali, Hindi And Assamese
Nagaland	Bengali	Hindi And Nepali
Mizoram	Bengali	Hindi And Nepali
Tripura	Bengali	Hindi
Meghalaya	Bengali	Hindi And Nepali
Manipur	Manipuri	Nepali, Hindi And Bengali
Orissa	Oriya	Hindi, Telegu And Santali
Maharashtra	Marathi	Hindi, Urdu And Gujarati
Gujarat	Gujarati	Hindi, Sindhi, Marathi And Urdu
Daman And Diu	Gujarati	Hindi And Marathi
Dadra And Nagar Haveli	Gujarati	Hindi, Konkani And Marathi
Goa	Konkani	Marathi, Hindi And Kannada
Karnataka	Kannada	Urdu, Telugu, Marathi And Tamil
Andhra Pradesh	Telugu	Urdu, Hindi And Tamil
Kerala	Malayalam	None
Lakshadweep Islands	Malayalam	None
Tamil Nadu	Tamil	Telugu, Kannada And Urdu
Puducherry	Tamil	Telugu, Kannada And Urdu
Andaman And Nicobar Islands	Bengali	Hindi, Tamil, Telugu And Malayalam

Children in India often grow up with parents from different language backgrounds, or in a community with neighbours speaking different languages. For that reason, most Indian children speak more than one language before they enter school. Many Indian children, especially in the middle or upper classes, attend English medium schools, where the English language is taught in addition to much of the curriculum being taught in English. It is not uncommon for students to learn up to three different languages at once, and these languages are not restricted to only other Indian languages. French, German and Spanish are commonly taught throughout the country.

English is the language commonly used in business. Educated Indians have excellent English-speaking skills and are highly articulate. However, Indian English evolved during British rule and, as such, Indians speak the 'Queen's English' with some idiosyncrasies that might leave you scratching your head. Some words might seem foreign to you, or the pronunciation or syllable emphasis may leave you wondering what is being said.

With time you will soon be able to interpret the conversation with ease. A helpful hint in the learning process would be to ask how a word is spelled; this will give you many "Aha!" moments. A common example of syllable emphasis would be the word 'development'; nearly all Indians say 'develOPment', whereas Americans, for example, put the stress on a different syllable, saying 'deVELopment'.

Indians are notorious for speaking too quickly for foreigners. This usually has to do with not using pauses, as Indians don't pause after each phrase and barely pause at the end of a sentence. By simply asking someone to speak slower, it will make the communication flow with more ease.

While it's not necessary to know Hindi or the local language, at times it can be beneficial. Just knowing some of the basics is helpful for getting around, asking for help and knowing what people might be saying amongst themselves. Indian people are appreciative of the efforts of those who take an interest in their culture and express their delight with those who take the time to learn their language. Even a simple thank you in Hindi will bring surprise, appreciation and even some joyful applause. They are happy to teach their language and take great pride in doing so.

USEFUL HINDI PHRASES

English	Hindi Tranlation
Hello	Namasté/Namaskar
See you later	Baad mein milte hai
See you tomorrow	Kal milte hain
How are you	App kaise hai
I am fine	Main thik hu
Ok, Good, Fine (Colloquial)	Thik hai
What is your name	Aap ka kya naam hai
My name is _____	Mera naam _____ hai
Very nice to meet you (Formal)	Aapse milkar bahut acha laga
Nice to meet you too (Reply)	Mujhe bhi aap se milkar acha laga
Yes	Haan
No	Nahi
It's a pleasant day	Yeh ek sukhad din hai
Do you speak English	Kya apa English bolte hai
Is there someone here who speaks English	Kya yaha koi hai jo English bolta/bolti hai
Thank you for inviting me	Mujhe bulane ka shukriya
It was nice meeting you	Aapse milkar accha laga
I don't know Hindi	Mujhe hindi nahi aati hai
I don't understand	Mai samjha/samjhi nahi
Speak more slowly	Aur dhire se bolen
Come again?	Phir se aana?
Where are you from	Aap kaha se hai
You're very kind	Aap bahot dayaalu hain
India is a beautiful country	India ek khoobsurat desh hai
Big	Bada
Small	Chhota
Today	Aaj
Tomorrow	Kal

English	Hindi Tranlation
Not too spicy please	Tikha Kam karna please
Where is the toilet	Toilet kaha hai
How much is this	Ye kitnay ka hai
I'm from _____	Main _____ se hu
I live in _____	Main _____ mein rehta/rehti hun
Please	Kripiyaa
Thank you (Formal)	Dhanyavaad
Thank you very much (Formal)	Aapka bahut bahut dhanyavaad
Thank you (Colloquial)	Shukriya
You're welcome	Aap kaa swagat hai
Don't mention it, It's nothing	Koi baat nahi
Excuse me (To get someone's attention)	Suniye
Can you repeat that?	Phir se bolo?
Pardon me, I'm sorry	Maaf Kijiye
Good, Okay	Accha
Just one minute	Bas ek minute
I'm sorry	Mujhe maaf karein
Definitely!	Pakka!
Let's go	Chalo
Congratulations!	Badhai ho!
Excellent work!	Ati utkarasht kaam!
Water	Paani
Tea	Chai
Hello everyone, I'd like to welcome you	Sabhi ko Namaste, Main aap sabka swagat karta/karti hu
I am looking forward to creating a successful partnership	Main ek kamyaab saajhedaaree banaane ke lie utsuk hoon

HISTORY
OF INDIA

India is one of the world's oldest civilizations. Anthropologists and genetic scientists place modern man in India at least 70,000 years ago, as part of an eastward migration from Africa to Australia. Voluminous books could be written about the great dynasties and empires of India originating from villages along the Indus River (from which India draws its name) in what is now known as Pakistan. The history of India is richly varied and has been formed from many cultures which came in peace or in war to expand their empires. Indian history can be divided into three periods – ancient, medieval and modern.

CHRONOLOGICAL HISTORY

3300-1500 BC
Ancient Indus

1500-500 BC
Vedic Period

500-350 BC
Persian Empire

327-323 BC
Alexander the Great

322-185 BC
The Great Mauryan Empire

273-232 BC
Ashoka the Great

320-550 AD
The Golden Age of the Guptas

647-1200
The Classical Age of the North and South Kingdoms

1200-1500
The Delhi Sultanate and the Beginning of Colonization

1526-1761
The Great Mughal Empire

1542-1605
Akbar the Great

1600-1947
The East India Company and Colonial India

1940s
The Indian Independence Movement

1948-1991
Bharat's Birth Pangs

1991-Present
Bharat the Great

BRIEF TIMELINE OF ANCIENT INDIA

The beginning of the Indus Valley Civilization can be dated to 3000 BC. Harappa cities were established in 2500 BC. Around 2000 BC, the decline of the Indus Valley Civilization began. In 1600 BC, the Aryans drove away the Dravidians, making it their home. The use of iron tools began at around 1100 BC. The Rig Veda – believed to be holy scripture of ancient India – was composed during the second century BC. The Indo-Aryans conquered the whole of North India and ruled over 16 states. Later in 700 BC, the caste system started taking shape and declared Brahmans as the highest class. In 527 BC, Prince Siddhartha Gautama attained enlightenment and becomes Buddha, creating Buddhism, one of the major religions in India and abroad. Prince Mahavira founded Jainism in 500 BC. In the same period, the great Mauryan dynasty was on the rise, and the Gupta era saw its downfall in 528 AD.

BRIEF TIMELINE OF MEDIEVAL INDIA

In 1290 AD, the sultan Jalal ud-din Firuz established his sultanate in Delhi and thus began the rule of the Mughal Empire in India. In 1343 AD, the southern kingdom built the capital at Vijaynagar, taking over the Mughal sultanate of Madura. Babur invaded India in 1497, with his son taking over the kingdom after his death in 1530.

Akbar then became king and was considered one of the greatest rulers of medieval India with a very prosperous kingdom from 1556 to 1605. His son Jahangir succeeded him. A few years later in 1611, foreigners began travelling to India to trade, including the British East India Company, who established their empire in India. In 1627, a Hindu king, Shivaji of the Maratha Kingdom, established a presence in the northern and western parts of India. Construction of the Taj Mahal began in 1631, during the period of Shah Jahan. However, in 1658, Shah Jahan's son, Aurangzeb, seized power, sending his father to exile. Aurangzeb died in 1701, ending the Mughal era.

BRIEF TIMELINE OF MODERN INDIA

In 1751, Britain became the dominant colonial power in India, defeating Siraj-ud-daulah and seizing control of the northern parts of India. Marathas had control over most of the northern and central regions of India during the 1760s. By this time, the British had become very powerful and controlled most of the southern region as well. In 1769, India saw a devastating famine that killed approximately ten million people in Bengal. In 1799, the British defeated Tipu Sultan in the south and took over the administration of Mysore. In 1848, Lord Dalhousie became the first Governor General of India. The railway, telegraph and postal services were introduced in India in 1853.

These advances were the beginnings of modern India, igniting further developments. The British officially took over the Indian government and proclaimed the Queen of England as the Empress of India in 1858.

By then, the struggle for freedom had spread across the country and many of the Indian people were against British rule. It was in 1885 that the Indian National Congress had its first meeting. In 1912, the capital was shifted to Delhi from Calcutta. Led by Mahatma Gandhi, non-violent protests were made against the British, with the Quit India movement launched in 1942. In 1947, India gained its independence from the British and is now known as the Republic of India.

With the entry of a new millennium, India has experienced a great transformation in culture and global influence. India has become an economic powerhouse in the world. During the early 1900s, extensive financial reforms were made by the finance minister Manmohan Singh, leading to rapid economic growth. Singh became known as the Father of Indian Economic Reform and went on to be elected Prime Minister in 2004 and again in 2009.

Under the current leadership of Prime Minister Narendra Modi, there is a clear agenda for economic reform, which includes reducing corruption and bureaucratic red tape, as well as making India the location of choice for foreign companies.

GOVERNMENT AND POLITICS

As the largest democracy in the world, India's success and opportunities lie in the stability of its government. With progressive policies having been put in place in the last five years during Prime Minister Modi's administration, the country is hoping to continue its growth which on average has been 7.4% going into the 2019 elections held in April and May.

India's 2019 election marks the 17th Lok Sabha (House of The People). The Lok Sabha Election Results 2019 led to the re-election of Prime Minister Narendra Modi for another five years and the BJP holding the majority of the seats in Lok Sabha.

THE TWO PRIMARY POLITICAL GROUPS ARE:

- Bharatiya Janata Party (BJP) led by Prime Minister Narendra Modi.
- India Congress Party (Congress) led by Rahul Gandhi.

Both groups have historically led aggressive election campaigns and between them represent a large majority of the people. While regional groups exist and certainly are important, these two groups have been at the forefront of India's democratic political process.

The National Congress, otherwise known as Congress, was the first party to have ruling privileges after partition, an event that divided the country between India and Pakistan.

The BJP was created to represent India's 'Hindutva'. It has used digital methods to promote its messages, much like the Obama Administration in the US.

The BJP's Modi is seen as a global leader and is respected in the international community.

The BJP's initiative in the last five years has been to show the world that India is a force with which to be reckoned. India has more to offer the world than just 'outsourcing'; it has a workforce of intelligent and innovative youth and is a country that can offer a home to new global startups and entrepreneurs willing to take on the challenges of creating a company in India. India is forming a hub of businesses which can grow to be counted upon the lists of global unicorns.

The BJP is credited with the following programmes that promote foreign investments and make it easier for global entrepreneurs to set up and do business in India.

- **INVEST INDIA**: The Invest India programme was launched to help organize existing infrastructure for large companies to SMEs and offer a one-stop platform to easily find funding, tax incentive programmes and strategic partnerships with regional government, as well as help with the transition of entering the market in India. Invest India also helps companies with the incubation process. Ideal for large- to medium-size businesses.

- **STARTUP INDIA**: Allows for an easy process of incorporation and learning local government policies to help you find local partners within India. We recommend you study this site as it can also help you understand what products and services can be offered, but also offers you the opportunity to find local partners. Startup India was created to make it easy for early-stage companies.

- **MAKE IN INDIA**: An initiative launched in 2014 to help improve and bring back the development and creation of jobs in manufacturing. The programme offers incentives to companies both locally and globally to create factories and satellite locations that create jobs in these areas. When the programme launched it allowed India to become the leader in foreign direct investments, surpassing the US and China. India emerged with $230 billion in investment commitments in 2014 when the programme launched. The programme also allows for 100% Foreign Direct Investment. Because of the programme, India's relationships with both Japan and South Korea have seen tremendous growth as both countries have created bilateral initiatives to push growth in the 25 areas of focus under the programme.[1] This led companies like Samsung to enter the market more aggressively and Samsung now has the largest mobile phone factory in the world in the city of Noida, making its devices and exporting them. The factory opened in June 2018 and manufactured devices are expected to grow from 65 million to 120 million units per year once its final phases are completed. The Make in India programme has been integral in improving the 'ease of business' ranking of India.

The current government also helped launched the government think tank NITI Aayog, a pro-industry group led by Amitabh Kant. The think tank invites entrepreneurs, industry leaders and individuals to help solve India's more pressing issues in relation to water, alternative energy, farming and new technology that incorporates AI, blockchain, digital payments and can help in the goal of seeing both smart cities and smart villages emerge throughout the country.

For further information on recent election results, visit the Parliament of India, Lok Sabha website. This resource will help you understand the various policies being put in place and the problems facing the government that need entrepreneurs and industry experts to support growth and find solutions.

PART 3

CULTURE: SOCIETY, HIERARCHY AND RELIGION

CULTURE
AND SOCIETY
OVERVIEW

India welcomes business partners from all over the world, but business is done differently in India than in much of the world. While Indian business looks and feels Western in many ways, with English widely spoken as one of India's official languages and business attire resembling that on Wall Street or the financial hubs of London, India retains a uniquely Eastern character. An understanding of the country's history, culture and traditions is essential in achieving a successful business partnership in India.

India is an extremely vibrant and diverse country steeped in complex history with various religions, traditions and ethnicities. The cultural information in this book is the result of personal experience and research. It has been said that it would take two lifetimes to understand the Indian culture. Some would argue that two lifetimes wouldn't suffice, as even within a single community there are various languages and foods, as well as different beliefs and views of Indian culture, tradition, history and religion. However, a few things seem to be universal: a strong sense of community and the undeniable importance of families and personal relationships are a prevalent anchor within India's culture and society.

Indians have mastered the art of a warm welcome, and while the Indian people take great pride in their rich historical and spiritual traditions, they simultaneously are open to the influx of Western culture and influence.

The game 'Snakes and Ladders' was invented in India in the 13th century by a poet named Saint Gyandev. The ladders represent the virtues while the snakes indicate vices. The game was initially invented as a moral lesson about karma to be taught to children. During British rule of India, this game made its way to England and was eventually introduced in the United States of America by game-pioneer Milton Bradley in 1943.

HIERARCHY
IN SOCIETY

Hierarchy is inescapable in India. From the caste systems to interactions with more formal sophistication, it's of great importance to recognize the role hierarchy plays in India's social and business relations.

Indians were highly influenced by the 200-year British rule and as such practice a higher level of formality between colleagues than their Western peers. You might not be able to initially see the difference in the hierarchy when you walk into any environment, but Indians can. From birth, Indians are made conscious and aware of social order and their status relative to other people, whether they are family, friends or strangers.

This British influence remains visible; for example, it is common to use the salutations 'sir', 'madam' or 'ma'am' when addressing someone new, or when talking upwards in seniority or status. It would be considered highly inappropriate to address someone you've just met by their first name. It is recommended to use last names upon meeting someone for the first time and mention any higher academic or occupational titles.

Within the home, there is an established hierarchy as well, albeit practiced to varying degrees and circumstances. In highly traditional rural areas, where the patriarchal hierarchy is very much still observed, wives will not address their husband by name as a sign of respect. Women must keep their head and face veiled when in the presence of an elder male. A new daughter-in-law is expected to move into her husband's family home to cook, clean and care for the daily needs of the entire family. She is sometimes not allowed to eat with the family and not allowed to sit when in the same room as her in-laws.

Not all Indian households are bound by these strict, compulsory expressions of hierarchy. Homes closer to urban areas or with higher education levels have more relaxed standards of hierarchy. Some practices, however, still seem to be universally practiced at different levels.

Conditioned since childhood to show honour and respect, children are taught not to address elders or seniors by their first name only. When addressing an elder, the suffix 'ji' (Hindi) is added to convey honour and respect. For example, if someone's name is Pravin, and we want to show respect, we would call him Pravin-ji. Children will also address their parents in this manner, for example, the father may be called Papa-ji rather than just Papa or Mama-ji rather than just Mama. Teachers in India are highly revered and believed to be gurus. Students are taught to stand when a teacher enters a room and often address them as Master-ji or Guru-ji.

Children are also taught the age-old tradition of touching the feet of elders, considered to be a mark of respect. This gesture can be seen in almost all Hindu families, both in India and abroad.

Outside the family, hierarchy and respect in the community are often acknowledged using respectful titles with elder neighbours and acquaintances, such as 'Uncle', 'Aunt or Auntie'. 'Brother' or 'Sister' is also universally extended to acquaintances or those met in passing, such as shopkeepers, even when they are not a family relation. Juniors yield to seniors by offering a seat on a crowded bus or train, stand when a senior enters a room and open doors for them. Some will refrain from smoking or drinking alcohol in their presence, even on special occasions. They will speak humbly and politely; they are slow to disagree and will often withdraw from a situation that is likely to lead to a confrontation.

The influences of Hinduism and the ancient tradition of the caste system have created a culture that emphasizes established hierarchical relationships. The caste system was originally a Hindu concept, but is now practiced by nearly all Indians within many religions. Castes or categories were originally based on occupations referring to a distinct and rigid social order dictating values and life possibilities and passed down the family line. One's identity, educational and vocational options, and acceptable life connections are all determined by the caste and family into which one is born.

Kumbh Mela is the world's largest gathering of humans. Kumbh Mela is a mass Hindu pilgrimage of faith in which Hindus gather to bathe in a sacred or holy river. This event is held every 12 years and is considered the largest event in the world. An estimated 120 million people visited Kumbh Mela in 2013 in Allahabad over a two month period including over 30 million on a single day on 10 February 2013.

INDIA'S CASTE SYSTEM

Brahmins
Priestly, academic class

Kshatriyas
Rulers, administrators, warriors

Valshyas
Artisans, tradesmen, farmers, merchants

Shudras
Manual laborers

Dalits/Untouchables
Street cleaners, menial tasks

The caste system is one of the most divisive social and political issues facing India today. Understanding its basic structure and relevance to society will ease many of your business interactions. Westerners wonder what effect the caste system will have in doing business in India. The answer depends largely on which Indian you ask. Some Indians, especially the younger generations, will insist that the rigid hierarchy of caste is no longer of any importance, and that may be true, at least for their generation. Many others, including from that same young generation, will insist that caste is still very important and affects many aspects of daily life. Some Indians have even modified their names to make their caste unrecognizable.

While caste is fading as a major influence in Indian life and in the workplace, it has hardly disappeared. Indians have a natural radar, scanning for clues that indicate where they fit into the puzzle that is the caste system. Even for those who place lesser value on caste protocols in daily life, when important life decisions such as marriage must be made, the importance of caste becomes very evident.

Westerners are not likely to notice the part caste plays in contemporary Indian life since Westerners don't know the complexities of how the caste system works. Westerners, however, are also affected by the caste system without even knowing it. That is not in the sense of having restrictions put upon them, but, by simply being outside the caste system, Westerners are sometimes considered 'outcasts'.

Westerners are likely to find certain caste-driven behaviours unfair, baffling or incomprehensible. They might wonder, for example, why a certain Indian is selected or promoted when another is clearly more qualified, why a hard-working student scoring higher on a university entrance exam is rejected and another getting a lower score is accepted instead, why certain team members always make the coffee while others simply enjoy it when served, why some Indians help move tables and chairs around the office as others sit idly by. In India, these could all be caste-related behaviours, but a Westerner would not know this and might impose a less than kind explanation for these actions.

It is important to consider that Westerners also exhibit similar behaviours in their own societies with both spoken and unspoken hierarchies. Attitudes in action and words are extended based on occupation, ethnicity, socio-economic status, education levels, skin colour, sexual orientation, religious beliefs, political views and family-taught prejudices. All of these play a role in daily life in society and affect one's position and place in the world.

RELIGION

India is known throughout the world for its history of religion and spirituality. Much of India's culture is deeply intertwined and cultivated from the guiding force of its religious practices and traditions. Religious beliefs and rituals are very important in the lives of many Indians and contribute to the core fundamentals of social life.

India is the birthplace of four of the world's major religions: Hinduism, Buddhism, Sikhism and Jainism. These four religions are linked by their belief in *samsara*, the idea that the cycle of birth, life, death and rebirth is the destiny of every living thing. (The traditional Hindu vegetarian diet is the logical conclusion of this belief in reincarnation.) These religions also share the belief in the moral law of cause and effect called *karma*, that one's actions and thoughts in past lives determine their fate in present and future lives.

Within India, the majority of people follow Hinduism, accounting for 79.8% of the population. Islam is the second-largest religion with 14.2%. Other major religious groups in India are Christians, making up 2.3% of the population, Sikhs at 2%, Buddhists at 0.8% and Jains with 0.4%.

The Constitution of India declares that the nation is secular in nature, but that the right to freedom of religion is fundamental. While the government disallows religious discrimination, tensions between religious communities, most prominently between Hindus and Muslims, continue to plague the country.

Devout Hindus are likely to engage in daily *pujas*, which is the sacred practice of revering gods or goddess through prayer and ritual. It is very common for religious Indian households to have a small altar with small statues of gods and goddess in their homes. It's also common to see these altars along the roadsides, tucked into alcoves inside schools and government buildings, in hotels and inside a merchant's place of business. At the start of a business day, it is common to see Hindus pray to Ganesha, the elephant-headed deity believed to be the remover of obstacles, or to Lakshmi, the goddess of wealth, fortune and prosperity.

Similarly, the Islamic call to prayer five times daily commonly emanates from local mosques. India is home to the third-largest Muslim population in the world, resulting in much of India's iconic architecture, the most notable examples being the Taj Mahal, Agra Fort, Delhi Fort and the Qutub Minar.

India holds an important role in early Buddhism as it was at Sarnath, just outside of Varanasi, where Buddha preached his first sermon, establishing Buddhism by "setting in motion the wheel of truth."

Christianity has been in India for 2,000 years, introduced by Thomas, one of the 12 Apostles of Jesus. Christian missionaries have not only contributed to the growth of Christianity in India, but also to the development of education, literacy, health and medicine.

There is a common misconception that all Indian men wear a turban. While it is common to see a Hindu groom wear a turban on his wedding day, it is the men of the Sikh faith who wear a turban daily when in public. An identifying article of faith for Sikhs is to maintain uncut hair, for both women and men. Sikhs are not to cut hair from any part of their bodies, which is why a Sikh man will have a long beard and long hair.

Karma is the foundation of Jainism. Believing that the soul is made pure by good deeds, faith and knowledge, Jains conquer worldly desires through abstinence and asceticism and follow a life of nonviolence. Devout Jains cover their mouths with a mask and clear their path with a small broom so that they do not inadvertently kill insects while breathing or walking.

India is abundant with temples of every faith. Temples of every faith soar with architectural grandeur or humble simplicity, all steeped in rich history. Religion must always be treated with respect in India and any deviance from the established norms is sure to cause offense. Women and men are expected to not expose their shoulders or legs when inside places of worship. Upon entering religious sites, whether it be a temple, a mosque or a shrine, shoes are removed. Sikh gurudwaras and mosques require both men and women to cover their heads when inside. This can be with a scarf, a shawl or any other type of cloth. Scarves are often available onsite, free for visitors, to ensure the strict dress code is followed.

In Jain temples, leather goods such as shoes, belts or wallets are not permitted. In many Jain and Hindu temples, all women of menstruating age, usually ages 10-50, are not permitted inside. Mosques are segregated and non-Muslims are not usually allowed inside during prayer time. In addition, photography of deities or inside religious sites is often discouraged and deemed offensive to those taking part in prayer and worship.

Rivers are considered sacred by some religions in India. For Hindus specifically, the water of the Ganges River, or Mother Ganga, is considered sacred and is said to have purifying powers. For this reason, Hindus come to the Ganges River to cleanse the body and mind, as bathing in the river is believed to cause the remission of sins. It is also believed that when the ashes of a loved one are scattered into the pure waters of the Ganges, this will facilitate *moksha*, or liberation from the cycle of life and death. Paradoxically, as a result of this sacred ritual, the Ganges has become one of the dirtiest rivers in the world.

WELL-KNOWN INDIANS

Indians take great pride in their heritage and of the people who helped to create its richness and variety in global recognition. The history of the Indian people goes back to the Indus Valley Civilization. Since then, there have been many Indians who have left their lasting legacy in different fields, be it in philosophy, science, the arts, culture or sports. Indians appreciate foreigners taking interest in their hailed heroes and are genuinely surprised and happy when they are brought up in conversation. Here are just a few examples of some of India's modern-day leaders and stars that would be a great icebreaker to creating a valuable connection with a colleague or acquaintance.

BUSINESS

MUKESH AMBANI is a business tycoon, Chairman of Reliance Industries Limited (RIL) and is ranked amongst the richest people in the world. He is the richest person in India and is considered to be one of the world's most powerful personalities. His brilliance and success are illustrated by the fact that his company is currently India's second most valuable by market value.

ISHA AMBANI is a businesswoman and the daughter of Mukesh Ambani. She became a member of the board of directors of Reliance Jio and Reliance Retail in 2014. In December 2015, she and her twin brother, Akash, introduced the Jio 4G network service. That year, *Forbes* named her on its list of 'Asia's Power Businesswomen 2015: 12 To Watch'. At the 2016 Lakme Fashion Week, she launched the online fashion retailer, AJIO, a subsidiary of Reliance Retail.[1]

SUNDAR PICHAI is a computer engineer and the current CEO of the technology giant Google. Pichai received his education from some of the most prestigious institutions in the world. He joined Google in 2004 as a product manager and led the innovative efforts for several of Google's products, including Google Chrome and Chrome OS. Eventually, he took over the management of Google products, Gmail and Google Docs, and rose rapidly through the ranks.

RATAN TATA is one of the leading Indian industrialists, and former chairman of the largest Indian multinational conglomerate, Tata Group. He currently holds the post of Chairman Emeritus of Tata Sons, the holding company of the Tata Group, which controls some of its major companies, including Tata Steel, Tata Motors, Tata Power, Tata Consultancy Services, Indian Hotels and Tata Teleservices.

MEDIA AND ENTERTAINMENT

PRIYANKA CHOPRA is a film actress and singer who has emerged as one of the most popular and high-profile celebrities in India. Born to physician parents, she was schooled in different cities across India until the age of 13, when she was sent to the US to pursue her higher education. Upon returning to her homeland, she was selected to represent India at the Miss World pageant, where she was crowned 'Miss World 2000'. After winning, she left her studies to join the film industry. Chopra has starred in numerous box-office successes and television series. She is married to American singer-songwriter Nick Jonas.

AMITABH BACHCHAN is a famous actor, who started out by starring in Hindi movies and gradually moved on to act in Malayalam and English films. He gained so much popularity during his career that the famous French director, François Truffaut, named him a 'one-man industry'. Not only has he acted in serious action movies, but has performed in a variety of roles in comedy and drama. Bachchan is the recipient of three 'National Film Awards' and the Indian government has conferred upon him the 'Padma Shri', 'Padma Bhushan' and 'Padma Vibhushan' awards for his exceptional contribution to world cinema.

SALMAN KHAN is a film actor, producer, singer and television personality. In a film career spanning almost 30 years, he has received numerous awards, including two 'National Film Awards' and two 'Filmfare' awards. He is known well beyond India and cited as one of the most commercially successful actors in Indian cinema. According to the *Forbes 2018* list of 'Top-Paid 100 Celebrity Entertainers' in the world, he was the highest ranked Indian for the third time in a row.[2]

VIDYA BALAN is an actress known for pioneering a change in the portrayal of Hindi film heroines with her performances of strong-willed women. She is the recipient of several awards, including a 'National Film Award', six 'Filmfare' awards and six 'Screen Awards'. She was awarded the 'Padma Shri' by the Indian government in 2014. In addition to acting in films, Balan promotes humanitarian causes and supports the empowerment of women.

MUSICIANS

YO YO HONEY SINGH is a music director, songwriter, Indi-pop singer, music producer and film actor. Known as the Indian 'King of Rap', his music is popular at weddings and wherever a party is happening. He started as a session and recording artist and became a bhangra music producer. Singh is now producing music for Bollywood films.

ARIJIT SINGH is a musician, singer, composer, producer and music programmer. He sings predominantly in Hindi and Bengali but has also performed in various other Indian languages. Singh often lends his voice to India cinema soundtracks. He is regarded as one of the most versatile and successful singers in the history of Indian music and Hindi cinema.

LEADERS

MAHATMA GANDHI was a lawyer who became the primary leader of India's independence movement. He led India to independence from British rule but also inspired movements for civil rights and freedom across the world. Best remembered for his dedication to non-violent means of civil disobedience, he led Indians in the 'Dandi Salt March' to protest against the British-imposed salt tax and launched the 'Quit India Movement', a mass protest demanding "an orderly British withdrawal" from India. He is known in India as 'The Father of the Nation', or *Bapu*. He also campaigned for women's rights, religious tolerance and reduction of poverty. Mahatma Gandhi was tragically assassinated in 1948 by an extremist who opposed Gandhi's doctrine of nonviolence.

MOTHER TERESA, clad in a white, blue-bordered saree, is a symbol of love, care and compassion. Known the world over, Mother Teresa was an Albanian-born Indian citizen who lived to serve the unwanted, unloved and uncared-for people of the world. Founder of the 'Missionaries of Charity', with her fervent commitment and incredible organizational and managerial skills, she developed an international organization with a passion for helping the impoverished. For her service to humanity, she was honoured with a Nobel Peace Prize in 1979. She was canonized by Pope Francis on 4 September 2016.

PARAMAHANSA YOGANANDA is regarded as one of the foremost spiritual figures of modern times. Even as a child, he seemed to be more aware of the spiritual self than was considered usual. Native to India, this guru emigrated to the US where he taught and practiced spirituality for over three decades. He earned the respected title of 'Father of Yoga' in the US, where he founded the Self-Realization Fellowship (SRF) to disseminate his teachings on India's ancient spiritual practices. He spent the rest of his life teaching in the US.

SADHGURU JAGGI VASUDEV, often referred to as Sadhguru, is a yogi and mystic who founded the 'Isha Foundation', a non-profit organization which offers yoga programmes around the world. A multifaceted personality, he is also an author, motivational speaker and philanthropist, along with being a spiritual master. A spiritual experience at the age of 25 made him rethink his life's purpose and, eventually, he realized that his calling was to become a yoga teacher. He teaches worldwide with wisdom and endearing humour.

MATA AMRITANANDAMAYI, lovingly called Amma, Ammachi, or Mother, is a Hindu spiritual leader of international standing. Also known as the 'Hugging Saint', she is known to hug and bestow her unconditional love on people from all walks of life. She spent her childhood taking care of her family, dedicating all her chores to Lord Krishna, and it was through this selfless devotion that she gained the highest knowledge. She formed the international charitable organization Mata Amritanandamayi Math, with branches in 40 countries, working for the upliftment of the local people, fighting hunger, empowering women and opening schools and institutes of higher education.

ATHLETES

VIRAT KOHLI is an international cricketer and one of the top sportsmen in India. Considered to be amongst the best batsmen in the present era, he also doubles up as an occasional right-arm medium-pace bowler. He is known for his dependable and powerful batting style and has single-handedly won several matches for India. He plays for Royal Challengers Bangalore in the Indian Premier League (IPL) and has been the team's captain since 2013. Virat Kohli is married to famous Indian actress Anushka Sharma.

SACHIN TENDULKAR is a former international cricketer and a former captain of the Indian national team. He made his debut against Pakistan as a 16-year-old. In India, Sachin is more than a popular sportsperson; he is an institution unto himself. He is not just loved and respected but revered. Called the 'God of Cricket' by his fans, Sachin has ruled the game as an icon for over two decades and is widely considered to be the greatest cricketer ever.

PV SINDHU is a professional badminton player who earned widespread fame after winning a silver medal in the 2016 Rio Olympics. With this win, she became the first and youngest Indian woman to win an Olympic silver medal. She was also awarded the 'Padma Shri', India's fourth-highest civilian award, in 2015.

SANIA MIRZA is an Indian tennis star and one of the top doubles players in the world. Mirza burst onto the scene as a prodigiously talented teenage tennis star, winning several tournaments in the Indian local circuit before winning the 'Girls' Doubles' title at Wimbledon. A wrist injury shifted her game from singles events to doubles and mixed doubles tournaments, leading to her success in the Grand Slam tournaments. Her most fruitful partnership was with fellow Indian tennis star Mahesh Bhupathi in mixed doubles.

SCIENTISTS

SHAKUNTALA DEVI was a writer and mathematical genius popularly known as the 'human computer'. She was given this title after she demonstrated the calculation of two 13-digit numbers: 7,686,369,774,870 × 2,465,099,745,779, which were picked at random. She answered correctly within 28 seconds.

Born into an impoverished family in southern India as the daughter of a circus performer, she started displaying her skills at an early age. Her father recognized her as a child prodigy and took her on road shows where she displayed her effortless ability in calculation. She did not receive any formal education owing to her family's financial situation, yet emerged as one of the most brilliant international mathematical phenomena.

APJ ABDUL KALAM was a prominent scientist who also served as the eleventh president of India from 2002 to 2007. Renowned for his pivotal role in the nation's civilian space programme and military missile development, he was known as the 'Missile Man of India'. Kalam made significant contributions to India's Pokhran-II nuclear tests in 1998, which established him as a national hero. He served as the Chief Scientific Adviser to the prime minister in the 1990s. Immensely popular during his term, especially amongst the youth, he earned the moniker of the 'People's President'. He was honoured with several awards, including the 'Bharat Ratna', India's highest civilian honour, for his contribution to the nation's space and nuclear programmes.

CRIMINALS

PHOOLAN DEVI was popularly known as the 'Bandit Queen of India'. Once a hunted criminal, she transcended her life of crime to become a Member of Parliament. She was born into a poor household that considered girls a burden. She was married off at a very young age to a much older man. Her husband was a cruel and abusive man and Phoolan left him by running away and joined a gang of bandits. After many years with feuding gang members, the dangerous and dreaded Phoolan surrendered and spent 11 years in prison. After her release, she became a politician. Phoolan was shot and killed outside her Delhi bungalow in 2001 by Sher Singh Rana in revenge for the upper-caste men she had gunned down. Several films and documentaries have been made on her life story, *Bandit Queen* (1994) being the most notable.

DAWOOD IBRAHIM is a notorious gangster and hunted terrorist who is the mastermind of the 1993 Mumbai serial bomb blasts. Born to a Mumbai police constable, he began his criminal activities in his late teens, after being associated with the 'Haji Mastan' and 'Karim Lala' gangs. As a result of his famous falling out with the Haji Mastan, he formed his own gang, the infamous 'D-Company', in the 1970s. The gang indulges in drug and arms trafficking in more than 25 countries around the globe. Ibrahim was declared a 'global terrorist' by both the US and the Indian governments and is currently said to be residing in Karachi, Pakistan.

The Republic of India has two
principal names used in both
official and popular English usage,
each of which is historically
significant: 'India' and 'Bharat'.
A third name, 'Hindustan', is
sometimes an alternative name
for the region comprising most of
the modern Indian states of the
subcontinent when Indians speak
amongst themselves. The usage
of 'Bharat', 'Hindustan' or 'India'
depends on the context and
language of conversation.

PART 4

CULTURE: HOLIDAYS, CUISINE, ART AND MISCONCEPTIONS

NATIONAL HOLIDAYS AND FESTIVALS

India is a country of traditional and multicultural festivals and has more official holidays on its calendar than any other country in the world. Indians have been known to unabashedly declare that there are 365 days in the year and India observes 366 festivals and holidays. As a country rich with history, religion and culture, many social and religious festivals are observed every month.

People from each religion have their own cultural and traditional festivals, while some of these festivals are celebrated by people of all religions. Every festival is celebrated uniquely according to its rituals, beliefs and history. These festivals and holidays hold great significance in the lives of Indians. Some require complete closing of businesses, and as such it is important for those wanting to do business in India to understand the significance of these celebrations and sacred occasions.

Many foreign businesses struggle with India's holiday schedule. Indian federal and state governments have acknowledged a number of public holidays every month to accommodate over 1.3 billion people.

Although there are many ways to manage this schedule, most companies in India offer 10 to 14 public holidays, depending upon the company's past practices and industry norms. Many businesses in India close on gazetted holidays and grant employees several optional holidays they may select to observe on a non-gazetted holiday of their choosing. Gazetted holidays are occasions said by the government to be mandatory, while non-gazetted or restricted holidays are optional.

Irrespective of the policies of any company, industry or organization, whether they are public, private or multinational, there are three national public holidays when it is mandatory throughout India to remain closed:

- Republic Day – January 26
- Independence Day – August 15
- Gandhi Jayanti – October 2
  (Gandhi's birthday)

In addition to office closures, governments in the state and union territories often observe 'dry days', when the sale of alcohol is not permitted, on gazetted and state and union territory holidays. Dry days also routinely occur on local election dates.

It is important to note also that many young Indians may ask for leave for their marriage plans and events. Weddings in India are still mostly arranged and are a spectacular multifaceted occasion, the scope of which can span as many as seven days full of celebrations and ceremonies. With this much anticipated event comes much preparation; therefore, it is not uncommon for the engaged couple and their families to ask for up to three weeks leave. As modern business practices take root, it is becoming less common to ask for this lengthy time off, but be prepared for this inevitable situation.

It is important to check for any conflicts before scheduling travel dates, appointments and meetings etc. to ensure your plans will be fulfilled without disappointment. It's also important to mention that most of the festivals in India use independent religious calendars which are different from each other, as well as the standard Gregorian calendar, so the dates and duration of the festivals change from year to year. An excellent guide to when these holidays fall each year, as well as a brief description of each occasion, can be found on the 'Time and Date' website by searching for holidays in India.

Another excellent resource for finding holidays and dates by state and union territory can be found at the India.gov.in website by searching for the state and union territories holiday calendar.

INDIAN
CUISINE

Indian food is richly and widely diverse and considered an important element in bringing together friends and family. Food is an important part of Indian society. Events and celebrations such as birthdays, anniversaries and achievements are cause for a meal to emphasize the joyous occasion.

Indian cuisine has evolved from its origins due to the historical influxes of ancient foreigners such as the Persians, Greeks, Mongolians, Arabs, Turks and the Portuguese, as well as the influences of British rule. The ingredients and preparations of India food are wide with diversity depending on each region and its influences. Many people come to India to embark on a 'foodie tour', exploring the various food destinations and enjoying the scrumptious cooking styles of different regions.

Many foreigners associate Indian food as a singular cuisine with atmospheric levels of spiciness and an aroma generically described simply as 'curry', but this is far from the truth. Foreigners often use the word curry, but that doesn't make sense to an Indian. Curry is not a single spice, but rather a word originally invented by the British during their rule of India to describe an Indian sauce or gravy. However, with time, the word curry became more commonly known as a blend of spices typically consisting of turmeric, chili powder, ground coriander, ground cumin, ground ginger and pepper, and is made in mild, medium and hot strengths and what some call 'insane Indian hot and spicy'.

India is ranked top in the world for the highest percentage of vegetarians at 38% of its population. Most Indians observe this protocol because of strong religious beliefs. This is of utmost importance to many Indians and as such government food and safety standards require all packaged food products sold in India to be labeled with a mandatory mark in order to be distinguished as vegetarian or non-vegetarian. In many eating establishments vegetarian and non-vegetarian foods are not allowed to be served in the same space.

North Indian food is rich with dishes cooked in thick tomato, cream and yoghurt-based gravies. Flatbreads such as chapati, paratha and naan are a common accompaniment and often used as the 'utensil' to scoop up the dishes. The influence of the Mughal dynasty introduced luxurious ingredients such as cream, almonds and saffron.

The cuisine of the north is in sharp contrast to that of the south. Flavours in the south are simpler and key ingredients include coconut and tamarind. While sea-food is freshly abundant and renowned along the southern coast, the food in this region is still largely vegetarian. However, fish is the staple food of most who live in Bengal, along with heavy meat curries and rice. Similarly, meat-based dishes are predominant in the northeast, which is heavily influenced by the Tibetan and Nepalese cultures. In the cooler hill areas of India, thakpa (a clear, meaty noodle soup) and momos (Chinese-like dumplings filled with meats or vegetables) are popular choices.

The options are plentiful as to where to eat in India. You may have a hired domestic cook, but if you venture outside, the street food culture and variety of restaurants in India are abundant. Lining every sidewalk and alley you will find a variety of portable food stalls and drink stands. You'll also find roadside eateries serving the local renditions of vegetable dishes, sandwiches, samosa (a small triangular fried pastry traditionally filled with vegetables and spices) and snacks.

Dhabas are roadside pit stops for truck drivers and cater well to travellers wishing to take a break. It is said that the best dhaba is the one with the most trucks parked outside. International fast-food chains have gained popularity across the cities and towns of India. Major metropolitan cities have seen an explosion of foreign restaurants establishing themselves with a variety of international fares such as Chinese, Thai, Mexican, French and American.

The Indian subcontinent is home to over 70 different herbs and spices – but chilli isn't one of them. Chilli came from South America and was introduced to India by the Portuguese.

Foreigners will easily find familiar restaurant chains such as McDonald's™, KFC™, Subway™, Costa Coffee™ and Starbucks™, and these chains are likely to appear more and more in the years to come.

As with their savoury counterparts, Indian sweets vary throughout the country. It's no secret that Indians have a sweet tooth with an extraordinary variety of delectable desserts. Sweets are a warmly welcomed guest in any celebration of Indian life.

Gulab Jamun, deep-fried dumplings/doughnuts dipped in a rose-cardamom flavoured sugar syrup, is a must-serve dessert during the biggest festivals. Diwali simply wouldn't be the same without Ladoo, found in almost every sweet shop in India and made of a variety of ingredients, from coconut and dried fruit to chickpeas. Holi wouldn't be nearly as colorful without Gujia, a deep-fried dumpling filled with sweetened milk and dried fruits. Phirni and Kheer are creamy rice dishes made with fresh milk and other heavenly flavours such as pistachio and cardamom, and these are often featured on the celebrations of Eid and Ramadan along with Gajar ka Halwa, a mouth-watering preparation made with red carrots.

Other perennial favorites are Rasgulla (also called Paneer Balls), a spongy Bengali delicacy made with milk cheese and a light syrup. Mysore Pak is a very popular South Indian sweet made with chickpea flour, dry fruits, Indian ghee (clarified butter), sugar and cardamom. The taste is melt-in-your-mouth divinely delicious. The swirling artistry of Jalebi is a must-have as its one of the most popular sweets in all parts of the country. These are similar to funnel cakes, deep fried in pretzel or circular shapes and then soaked in sugar syrup.

As food and meals are an important part of Indian culture, there are certain rules of etiquette that should be observed and practiced.

Cows are considered sacred in Hinduism; therefore, the consumption of beef is considered taboo. In addition, Muslims refrain from eating pork as per religious beliefs. The sale of beef and pork in the majority of restaurants is seldom seen. Some communities within India allow beef to be sold and ordered in restaurants, especially in the south-west. In addition, international restaurants are increasingly including beef on their menus. Although McDonald's™

restaurants are a common sight in India, you're not going to find a traditional beef hamburger at any McDonald's™ restaurant anywhere in India.

Cleanliness is of great importance when preparing to eat a meal. Washing your hands before and after eating is expected, regardless of whether one is using cutlery or not. Eating Indian food with one's hands is a common practice and should only be done with the right hand. The left hand is considered unclean and is associated with going to the bathroom. Therefore, you should avoid your left hand coming into contact with food or with anything you pass to people.

There is a common belief that it is unclean to 'contaminate' another person's food or utensils with one's saliva. This is called 'jutha', meaning 'defiled'. This includes using someone else's eating utensils even momentarily, taking a bite from flatbread and passing it along or putting one's mouth on a common drink bottle. This is not usually true however for family members and close friends.

If you have read anything about travel to India, you have most likely heard of the phrase 'Delhi Belly'. This is an illness caused by the consumption of food or drink contaminated with bacteria. This is a common ailment for those who travel to India, but it doesn't need to be. Here are a few tips to help keep you away from any unwelcome trips to the bathroom:

- Only drink water that has been bottled or purified in homes or restaurants verified by a trusted source.
- If you are staying where there is no purified water from the tap, use bottled or purified water to brush your teeth as well.
- Beverages such as hot teas or coffee are usually safe.
- Packaged beverages such as sodas, juices, carbonated water, wine and beer are usually safe. Wipe off the top of any can or carton before opening.
- Avoid ice, unless you are sure it's made of safe water.
- Avoid raw foods, especially seafood. The exceptions are fruits and vegetables you have peeled or shelled yourself, or from a reputable eating establishment.
- Eat food that is thoroughly cooked and still hot when served.
- Boil unpasteurized milk before drinking it. Milk sold in markets in plastic pouches needs to be boiled before drinking.

ART, MUSIC, DANCE, BOLLYWOOD

India is art and art is India. The copious expressions of art crafted over millennia, from ancient to modern-day India, are evidence of the richness and beauty of India's cultural diversity. From its extraordinary architecture to woven silks, music and dance, painting and sculpture, literature, fashion and cinema, India provides a profusion of art to suit most anyone's appreciation and adulation.

ART

The origins of Indian art can be traced to prehistoric settlements where archeologists have found evidence of prehistoric rock art, consisting of carvings or drawings on cave rocks. The oldest examples are the Bhimbetka petroglyphs, found in central India and believed to be at least 290,000 years old. Cave paintings, representing animals and humans date from about 7,000 BC. The people of the Indus Valley Civilization produced the earliest known Indian sculptures, from between 2,500 and 1,800 BC. These were small terracotta and bronze figures, often depicting human and animal forms.

Indian art has had its cultural influences as well as religious influences such as Hinduism, Buddhism, Jainism, Sikhism and Islam. In spite of this complex mixture, the appreciation of each religion's art has been shared by people of all religions.

Early Buddhist artists created sculptures in stone and bronze in the 6th century BC. They also produced magnificent temples carved entirely in stone, decorated with Greek-influenced columns and sculptures.

According to Hindu beliefs, there are four goals in life each human should aspire to. Dharma, or righteous living; Artha, or wealth acquired through the pursuit of a profession; Kama, or human and sexual love; and Moksha, or spiritual salvation. These holistic views are reflected in many of the artistic representations of Hinduism.

Islam gained importance in India under the Mughal Empire, established in the 16th century. Artistic expression flourished under the Islamic rulers – it is during this time that the Taj Mahal was built. This jewel of Muslim art is a universally admired masterpiece of world heritage.

India became a British colony in the 19th century, making a monumental impact on Indian art. India's modern art is considered to have begun in Kolkata during this time. The British established new schools of art that promoted European styles and Europeans, who, in turn, had a growing fondness for Indian art. India's artistic influences can be found in home decor, clothing and accessories throughout the world today.

MUSIC

The music of India has a history spanning millennia and has evolved with every new century and generation. From classical and folk to rock and pop, to Hindustani and Carnatic, music has played an integral part in India's socio-religious life.

The early beginnings of music are evident at the site of the 30,000-year old Paleolithic and Neolithic cave paintings at the Bhimbetka rock shelters in Madhya Pradesh, which show music instruments and dancing. The Indus Valley Civilization produced 'Dancing Girl' sculpture (2500 BC) as well as ceramic art portraying men and women playing drums. The Vedic period of 1500-800 BC documents rituals of the performing arts written in the form of plays, along with 'tala', an ancient music concept traceable to the Vedic era texts of Hinduism and the singing of the Vedic hymns.

This evidence of singing and dancing and the playing of musical instruments exemplifies the deeply rooted appreciation and integral part that music plays in the daily rituals of Indian life and which continues today.

Every year, Chennai hosts the 'Music Season', highlighting and preserving Carnatic music associated with southern India. Spanning 20 weeks, this is the world's largest cultural event. The 'Music Season' allows aficionados of Carnatic music to appreciate performances by renowned artists, and promising young artists to display their talent. Many other forms of music with a rich history in modern-day India include Rabindra Sangeet, the music of Bengal, Uttarakhandi folk music, music associated with dance such as Lavani and Garba, as well as music from Rajasthan and Punjab. The list goes on and the message is clear – India and its music are inseparable.

DANCE

As with all Indian culture, Indian dance styles are widely varied and drawn from many influences. Indian dances are typically divided into classical and folk. Classical dances are usually spiritual in content and, while folk dances can share in this, these are dances of celebration. Indian dance is an expression of emotions; dances tell stories, they offer prayers and depict nature. Each dance style can be traced to different parts of the country, representing the culture and ethos of a particular region or a group of people.

Indian classical dance is often regarded as a form of worship and meditation. The most popular classical dance styles are Bharatanatyam from Tamil Nadu, Kathakali and Mohiniattam from Kerala, Odissi from Odisha, Kathak from Uttar Pradesh, Kuchipudi from Andhra Pradesh and Manipuri from Manipur. All of these styles use the 'mudras' (signs using the hand and fingers), which are also used in yoga as a common language of expression and were originally performed in the temples to entertain various gods and goddesses.

Indian folk and tribal dances are a product of different socio-economics and traditions. They are simple and are performed to express joy. Every day in India, there are multiple festivals and celebrations to be acknowledged. Folk dancing has become an integral part of the richness of Indian culture.

BOLLYWOOD

The name Bollywood is a combination of Bombay (Mumbai's original name) and Hollywood. These Hindi language films are the centre of the Indian movie industry. Bollywood movies have gained global popularity with their glamour and dazzle, colours and costumes.

Indians love their movies, so much so that they are willing to sit through a three- to four-hour Bollywood movie which includes an intermission. A Bollywood movie can include dozens of songs and dances, featuring as many as a hundred or more dancers. The characters played by India's dearly loved and highly revered actors usually tell the 'boy meets girl' story with lots of action, innocent coy smiles, high drama, playful humour and nearly always a happy ending.

Bollywood churns out over a thousand films per year and over 14 million Indians flock to them daily. Since the 1990s, the three biggest Bollywood movie stars have been the 'Three Khans': Aamir Khan, Shah Rukh Khan and Salman Khan, dominating the Indian box office. According to *Forbes*, Aamir Khan was "arguably the world's biggest movie star" as of 2017, due to his immense popularity in India and China.[1]

Other Hindi stars include Anil Kapoor, Madhuri Dixit, Akshay Kumar, Hrithik Roshan, Deepika Padukone, Ranveer Singh, Priyanka Chopra, Varun, Dhawan, Kajol, Anushka Sharma, Kareena Kapoor Khan, Amitabh Bachchan and Ranbir Kapoor.

Bollywood movies are not just about the story; the music in a Bollywood movie is just as significant. Composers in the Indian movie industry are equally as important as the directors, producers and actors.

Bollywood's international success has captured the attention of countries all over the world. People in Germany, Pakistan, the United Arab Emirates, Indonesia, Canada, the US and many countries in Africa and South America love Bollywood movies.

It is thought that henna, also called 'mehndi', originated in the deserts of India when the people living there discovered that covering their hands and feet with coloured paste from the henna plant helped them to feel cooler. It wasn't long until creative, intricate designs with the coloured paste began to be used. The complexity of designs grew and began to take on meaning. Eventually, brides began to decorate their feet and hands with henna as part of their wedding rituals.

STEREOTYPES AND MISCONCEPTIONS

Most of the world formulates its views of foreign countries through the lens of various media, such as news outlets, the internet, television and movies. As with any given medium of information and entertainment, the reality often lies somewhere in the middle of the varied extremes of events reported and cultures portrayed in print or on screen.

India is always making an impression of sorts. Headlines flash across news outlets representing India as progressing, admirable, inspiring and enticing. There are also stories that shed light on the less-than-favourable parts of India, and then there are the misconstrued conclusions or assumptions that are simply inaccurate. Over time, India has fallen prey to many stereotypes and misconceptions. An over-generalized belief or description of 'India' and 'Indians' is not a complete representation of India or its people. There is little that can be labeled generically as 'Indian culture'.

If you were to ask an Indian their perceptions of Westerners based on what they see in the news or in movies or in the cacophony of videos available online, they will likely respond that Westerners are, in their entirety, happy, wealthy and stress-free. That every weekend is spent partying and drinking with multiple sexual encounters. That their communities are crime- and corruption-free and that jobs are easily attainable for anyone and that no one lives on the streets. They believe the best healthcare in the world is available to all Westerners and is easily affordable.

Many also believe that all Westerners are liberal, selfish and overweight, that they don't have any family values or bonds, view marriage as a disposable commodity and that most are obnoxiously loud and rude. It is understandable, given their information sources, that many Indians have formulated a false narrative built around perceived notions of 'all Westerners' that creates barriers to understanding the realities.

India is peculiar to many Westerners simply because of its diversity, creating both inspiration and shock. Global news sources report the good, the bad and the ugly of any country along with the bizarre and even the contradictory. The following are a few examples of common stereotypes and misconceptions a foreigner might have about India and its society. Understanding the reality of Indian culture and society will help to clarify or discard any naïve assumptions, dispel any falsehoods, and hopefully help in an appreciation of the richness and diversity of India.

INDIANS ARE UNEDUCATED

In a country with a population as large as India's, it's inaccurate to make generalized assumptions about anything, including the education of an entire nation. Education is held in high regard in India and the notion that Indians are uneducated is incredibly inaccurate. As of January 2019, India had over 900 universities and 40,000 colleges. The literacy rate of India is approximately 75%, with variations between states. The state of Tripura has achieved a literacy rate of 94.65%, with Bihar as the least literate state at 63.82%.[1, 2]

Enrollment in higher education has increased steadily over the past decade, and India's improved education system is often cited as one of the main contributors to its economic development. Doctors and engineers top the list of professions in India, while MSs, MBAs and PhDs are all very common degrees. The university system in India is extremely competitive.

India is working to close the gap of the uneducated. Millions of children, mostly girls, are not attending school because of a lack of awareness and financial resources, and India has some distance to cover in catching up with the post-secondary education enrollment levels of developed nations.

INDIANS TALK FUNNY

Indian nationals abroad are sometimes met with the question: "If you are from India, how do you know how to speak English so well?" English is the second official language of India and is widely spoken across the country. Most schools, barring government schools and those for the underprivileged, are what is called an 'English Medium' school, which means their classes are taught in English.

While it's possible to navigate around the country with only English and no knowledge of any Indian language, miscommunication and confusion are bound to occur when conversing with Indians who might not use the language frequently, or when outside the concentrations of educated and working professionals. Conversely, with the influx of Western media influences such as television, movies and the internet into India, English references are spreading throughout different classes and regions.

An Indian accent is also often stereotyped or exaggerated. India was ruled by the British for 200 years, so it makes sense that Indians often have more of a British English accent as opposed to an American one. Indians also pronounce some words differently with the emphasis on different syllables. In addition, Indians often use words or phrases unfamiliar to Americans but common within British vernacular. The following are just a few examples that mean the same thing in theory but are used differently in the US, Canada, Europe, the UK and India, either as parallels or with entirely different meanings altogether.

> **QUEUE AND LINE:** Both are a sequence of people waiting their turn.
>
> **REPLY AND REVERT:** Both refer to answering a message, usually via email.
>
> **REACHED AND ARRIVED:** Both refer to you now being at your destination.
>
> **GASOLINE AND PETROL:** Both refer to the fuel necessary to drive a vehicle.
>
> **SCHEME:** One is a plan or programme meant to improve a situation, the other is a devious plan to do something wrong or illegal.
>
> **CRICKET:** One is the most popular sport in India, the other is an insect.
>
> **PASS OUT:** One means someone has successfully graduated or completed a study course, the other means to lose consciousness and faint.

As Western influence grows, so does the desire for many Indians to learn English to further their careers and personal lives. As with anyone learning a new language, patience and understanding are essential in supporting those continuing to learn a global language of business.

A point to consider is that those who speak with broken English know another language, something many English speakers can't say for themselves.

INDIANS SPEAK INDIAN AND HINDU

As a point of clarification, Hindu is a religion and Hindi is a language. Indians don't speak 'Hindu'; furthermore, Indians don't speak 'Indian' either. There are no such languages as Hindu or Indian.

It is important to know what languages are spoken in the areas you plan to work or visit. Even so, every region is different, and you might be met with a blank stare or confused expression from an Indian should you learn a few phrases in Hindi and go to a region that doesn't speak it. Hindi is largely spoken in Northern India and is likely to be only a second or third language for people of other regions.

ALL INDIANS ARE POOR

Although poverty is a pressing problem in India that cannot be ignored, there is a commonly held perception that all Indians are poor. This belief is perpetuated further by media portrayals of the country, such as in the movie *Slumdog Millionaire*. While it's true that 70.6 million Indians live below the poverty line, many in highly visible slums, this is not the case for the entire nation. The Indian nation holds a significant portion of the world's wealthiest people. According to *Forbes*, India is home to 101 billionaires, some of whom were "born with a silver spoon in their mouth", while many others started from the bottom and worked their way up to be esteemed business executives. India ranks fourth in the list of the world's billionaires, behind only China, the US and Germany.[3]

Life is quickly improving for the Indian people, especially within the middle class. Anirudh Krishna, professor of public policy and political science at Duke University in the US, defines middle-class as: "Freedom from vulnerability and a real chance of upward mobility." The Indian government defines any citizen who pays income tax as part of the middle class. The biggest increase in India's middle class comes mainly from the growth of the lower-middle class. While income levels are at odds with what is considered the middle and lower-middle-classes in the West, growth is indeed happening, with more Indians moving out of poverty and into more comfortable standards of living, with a real chance of upward mobility.

INDIA IS DIRTY AND CHAOTIC

The media often portrays India as a poor country of filth, stench and utter chaos. In a nation this size, with daily life for the most part still patterned on the routine of previous generations and an overburdened infrastructure, India has its work cut out for it with regard to order and cleanliness. India and chaos are in a sense synonymous. Seas of people, crammed trains and packed buses are everyday sights in India. The ways of life are the ways life functions in this organized chaos called India. You can expect confusion, disarray and maybe even some mayhem, but it's all part of the Indian experience. It might take some time to adjust to the rhythm of the madness, but if you surrender to the choreography of everyday life in India, savouring the moments as evidence of its extraordinary humanity, you'll be just fine.

THE COMMON MODE OF TRANSPORTATION ARE ELEPHANTS AND CAMELS

While it's not out of the ordinary to see an elephant or camel walking down the side of the road in India, this is hardly a common method of transportation to get to school, the office, the market or the shopping mall. Most Indians get around just like people in any other country, via car, motorcycle, public transportation, using on-demand transportation apps and good old-fashioned walking; with one exception. Indians have the added ease and thrill of having the option of using human or auto rickshaws to get around town. This option is even available through ride-hailing transportation apps such as Uber™ or India-based Ola™.

Merchants and farmers often use camels for work or transporting goods. Elephants are often used for circus acts and both are used for tourists to ride. A popular tourist attraction is to ride an elephant up the steep landscape to the gates of the Amber Fort in Jaipur. These elephants are decorated with traditional painted patterns. Approximately 100 elephants carry up to 900 visitors per day. This tourist favourite may end soon, due to the practice being under scrutiny for violating animal cruelty laws, as these elephants have been found to be forced to carry loads of more than the prescribed limits and to be suffering from health problems.

COWS FREELY ROAM THE STREETS OF INDIA

This one is true! Cows are considered sacred in the Hindu faith and are free to roam wherever they choose, and that choice is often to wander along the sides or in the middle of streets, roads, fields and beaches. Hindus do not actually worship cows as a deity, this is a common misconception, but they do deeply respect and honour cows for their gentle nature and for providing sacred gifts of nourishment in the form of milk and ghee (clarified butter).

These cows are basically harmless, but it is not advisable to approach them or touch them. Despite living in the constant presence of humans, they may feel threatened or spooked, or might be infected with disease. Some of these cows have owners and some do not. Many cities are taking measures to relocate them to safer living and eating environments.

WHERE ARE THE TOILETS AND TOILET PAPER IN INDIA?

In India, asking for or looking for 'toilet' signs will get you to where you need to go.

In India, you'll find two types of toilets, Indian and Western. Indian toilets, also known as Asian toilets or 'squatters', are the type that are flush against the floor with a hole and two footholds used in a squatting position, while a Western type has a bowl, a tank and a seat used in a sitting position.

Many health professionals claim that using a squatting position helps to maintain good colon health and lessen urinary tract infections. These health benefits aside, a foreigner might not feel comfortable using this effective yet unfamiliar method, so, in major cities, Western toilets in public places are becoming increasingly common and easily found.

Millions of Indians use water and their hand to clean themselves for both hygienic and environmental reasons rather than toilet paper, as is common in many Western countries. With the increased presence of Western toilets comes the increased presence of toilet paper, but even with this evolution, toilet paper is not always provided in public restrooms. For that reason, it is a good idea to have toilet paper with you, along with wet wipes and hand sanitizers as there may not be soap or towels available in some public places.

THE 'REAL INDIA' IS FOR HIPPIES

Many foreigners, naïve to the actual realities of the 'real India', are unaware of the many dichotomies the Indian experience offers. If you think India is for those who scurry to buy traditional Indian clothes like the 'real Indians' do, are experts at performing the 'downward dog' yoga position, live frugally, stay in cheap hostels, use public transportation, wear dreadlocks and chant spiritual incantations while searching for peace – and all with nothing but a backpack and spontaneity on their agenda – then you are right. Thousands of foreigners travel to India every year yearning for this experience and are fulfilled beyond their expectations.

If hiking the back paths within the natural wonders of India, or the zen of an ashram experience, or a 'come what may' attitude doesn't suit your fancy, there are other 'real India' experiences that would satisfy even the most sophisticated travel tastes. India offers every imaginable experience to any and all who travel to this extraordinary land. The most luxurious and internationally renowned hotels, shopping malls, designer stores to rival anything on Bond Street, Fifth Avenue or Rodeo Drive, nightclubs and restaurants are found in abundance. Traditional and modern lifestyles are evident through the dualities of Indian society, and as such, every imaginable experience is possible within India's rich and vibrant country.

There are many government 'clean India' initiatives in place alongside more education on the issues involved, with the aim being to clean up the roads, reinforce the infrastructure of cities and rural areas and promote individual social responsibility. The mind-boggling chaos goes hand-in-hand with the phenomenon of India, yet every day millions of India's people get from where they are to where they need to be.

INDIANS ONLY EAT CURRY

Indian food has become synonymous with curry. Indian food is multifaceted, diverse and reaches a far more sweet and savory palate beyond the generic curry. Every region of India has its own cuisine preferences complete with its own spices, preparations and presentations.

ALL INDIAN FOOD IS SPICY

Spices are widely used in Indian cuisine, especially cardamom, turmeric, cumin, coriander, mustard seed, ginger, saffron, nutmeg and clove. Just because a dish contains spices does not necessarily mean it will be hot. Restaurants catering to foreigners know that foreigners' levels of preferred spiciness may vary, and so adjust accordingly. Each region has its unique food, some more spicy, some less, and some not at all, so try them all; it might surprise you to find your new favourite in unexpected places.

ALL INDIANS ARE VEGETARIANS

Vegetarianism is often considered the benchmark of all cuisine in India due to its cultural and religious traditions, with 38% of the population identifying as vegetarian. Within India, vegetarianism varies greatly by religion and region. In states such as Rajasthan, the percentage of vegetarians is 74.9%, and in states such as West Bengal and Kerala, where meat or fish is prevalent, especially amongst Muslims, vegetarianism is as low as 1.4%.[4, 5]

ALL INDIAN WOMEN WEAR SAREES AND TUNICS AND MEN WEAR TURBANS AND SKIRTS

Not every woman in India wears a saree or tunic (a long top also called a 'kurti' or 'kurta') and not every man wears a turban or a skirt, called a 'lungi' (similar to a sarong, wrapped around the waist and usually extending to the ankles). While under British rule, Indian men shifted their dress style to match that of the British to allow for better career prospects. Even when the British left, the trousers stayed. Wearing Western clothes became a symbol of power and prestige within communities and in professional settings. By the 1950s, Western wear was the clothing style of choice for most men in India with the exception of extremely rural areas.

Women did not undergo the same clothing revolution. Even today, many women in small towns or villages are expected to honour their family by wearing traditional sarees or 'salwar kameez', an outfit comprised of a pair of trousers ('salwar') and a tunic ('kameez') that is usually paired with a scarf ('dupatta').

Women who live in major cities may choose to wear a variety of both traditional and Western styles, whether in business or casual settings. There are occasions, especially when attending high-profile events, where modern Indian women may choose to wear a traditional saree as a mark of deep respect for the Indian culture.

INDIAN WOMEN ARE SUBORDINATE TO MEN AND HAVE NO POWER IN SOCIETY

Despite being a strongly patriarchal society, as is common in developing countries, women are seen as being powerful alongside the gods. Hindus worship thousands of goddesses, and they believe that the goddess Shakti was the power who created the universe.

Traditionally women were expected to be the caregivers of the family, as wives and mothers, above any consideration of an occupation, education or career, as is reflected in the lower literacy rates amongst the female population. However, this idea is beginning to fade away, albeit largely within the upper and middle classes.

More women are attending university and going on to hold jobs and build careers outside the home, with an increasing number of women becoming entrepreneurs, CEOs, activists and philanthropists. The growing acceptance of female leadership and gender equality are helping to shape a competitive Indian economy and a more balanced home environment.

ARRANGED MARRIAGES
ARE FORCED

As many as 85% of marriages are still arranged in modern India. Families in India favour an arranged marriage over a 'love marriage', a union in which a couple falls in love and chooses to marry, as elders feel that exchanging wedding vows not only unites two souls together but unites two families. As a result, key family members, mediators and matchmakers play a crucial role in Indian nuptials. Indian unions are often based on caste, social and economic status, education, dowry and astrology.

In the past, neither the bride nor the groom was asked for their consent, and they typically met their spouse for the first time on the wedding day. In a modern arranged marriage, a potentially matched couple spends time getting to know one another before agreeing to the marriage. Rejections are common; not everyone marries the first person they meet. It is also increasingly common for two people to meet and start dating because of a mutual attraction.

Contrary to popular belief, dating is not a taboo in India. Some even go online to look for their life partner. If an attraction turns into a love affair and the topic of marriage arises, the majority of young Indians prefer to marry someone accepted by their parents, so the couple will arrange for the parents to meet and hope for their blessing.

INDIANS ARE NAZI SUPPORTERS?!

It may shock most visitors to observe the swastika symbol so predominantly displayed throughout India. However, before the symbol was made synonymous with the terrors of the Nazi regime in the 1930s and 1940s, the swastika was, and remains, an auspicious symbol widely used in many Asian countries to invite good fortune.

The word swastika is derived from the Sanskrit, meaning 'good fortune' or 'well-being'. The symbol appears to have first been used in Eurasia, as early as 7,000 years ago. To this day, the swastika is a sacred symbol in Hinduism, Buddhism and Jainism, and is commonly painted on the entrances of temples and homes in India and Indonesia to welcome health, luck, success and prosperity. The swastika is often used as a mandala for rituals such as weddings or welcoming a newborn. It is also found marked on financial statements, as it is thought to be conducive to wealth and prosperity.

INDIAN SOCIAL PHENOMENA

MULTIGENERATIONAL LIVING ARRANGEMENTS

Indian culture considers the family to be the core of society and families are typically communal in their living arrangements. 'Home' can be one large, single room or a multi-storied marble mansion, but most Indian homes are a multi-generational dwelling. This unique extended familial system has prevailed in India for centuries and consists of multiple generations of family living together under the same roof, with the eldest male as the head of the family usually having the greatest influence on family decisions.

PARTS OF THE BODY AND THEIR SIGNIFICANCE

Particular parts of the body have significant meaning that should be recognized and remembered when visiting or working with Indian nationals. The rigidity of these rules varies from individual to individual but as a whole are commonly observed across the country.

The right and left hand have very distinct functions in Indian culture. The right hand is used for eating and shaking hands, while the left hand is used for 'unclean' actions such as wiping yourself after using the toilet, cleaning your feet or removing your shoes. Pointing with your finger is also rude in India. If you need to point at something or someone, it's better to do so with your whole hand.

Feet are considered to be unclean and therefore it's important to avoid pointing your feet at people or touching people or objects (particularly books) with your feet or shoes. If you accidentally do so, you should apologize straight away.

The profound contradiction, however, is the Indian practice of touching the feet of elders or those held in high esteem. This act is an expression of deep respect for the age, experience, achievements and wisdom of the person whose feet are being touched. Indians believe that when a person bows down and touches the feet of their elders, their ego is suppressed.

In turn, the elder would then touch the person's head and may bless the person touching their feet. Grandparents, for example, would bless a grandchild with a long life, good health and a prosperous future. A teacher or mentor might say to a student "May God give you wisdom to do right." As a foreigner, you could offer these words: "Bless you" or "God bless you."

THE OBSESSION WITH FAIR SKIN

Indian markets sell a plethora of products designed to 'lighten' skin. The global skin lightening business is worth millions. Television commercials and social media praise the status of fair-skinned beauties and marriage website profiles are abundant with prospective brides and grooms "seeking a fair-skinned" significant other. India is obsessed with 'fair, light, or white' skin, favouring it over the naturally pigmented complexion of the subcontinent's natives.

Indians find it quite unfathomable to learn that people in other countries pay to have their skin shade appear darker with tanning spas and skin-darkening products. There are some signs of the obsession being rejected through prominent celebrity figures who are refusing to endorse this cultural phenomenon.

LADIES ONLY COMPARTMENTS AND SEPARATE QUEUES

In the Delhi Metro system, designated carriages of each train are labeled 'Ladies Only Compartments', providing women an option to travel with women only while using the metro transportation system.

In airports, malls, markets and monument entrances, women are routinely segregated from men, having separate queues.

These practices stem from safety issues and concerns or long-standing cultural traditions.

CRICKET: NOT JUST A SPORT, IT'S MORE LIKE A RELIGION

Cricket dominates India's sporting realm and social life. If there is a cricket match going on, you can be sure that much of the country will be gathered around a TV or radio cheering on their team. Hockey is the 'official' national sport, however cricket can accurately be deemed the 'real' national sport.

No matter which part of India you visit, you will find roadside cricket matches, rural village matches and entire television channels dedicated solely to the sport of cricket. It is no wonder cricket is affectionately known as a 'religion' to many Indians.

Cricket is the fastest way of befriending an Indian. Cricket is often a great conversation topic and if you have the opportunity to watch a cricket match live, it is a must-do experience to see the intense enthusiasm with which Indians regard this lively sport.

The Indian cricket team has been world champion twice, in 1983 and 2011, and were runners-up in 2003.

INDIA'S DOMESTIC HELP

It's exceedingly common within middle- to upper-class Indian homes to have maids, servants or housekeepers employed to help with daily domestic chores such as cleaning, cooking and looking after children or elderly family members. This employment can also extend to private drivers and gardeners.

The population of India is so large that sufficient jobs are required to support its citizens. Domestic chores that Westerners often do themselves are most often hired out in India and, due to the large income inequality gap in the country, the employment of domestic help is a common occurrence. For those that can afford it, it's a rarity not to have domestic help.

There are domestic home help and driver staffing agencies who specialize in assisting foreigners find the right help, considering several factors such as good English-speaking skills and background screening and identity verification to alleviate security risks.

A NAME IS NOT JUST A NAME

Indian names are uniquely special because they have deep meaning and significance to each individual. Western names such as Sarah or John are typically names given at birth by the parents based largely upon the fact that they simply like the name, or it might have some familial significance.

Popular Indian names such as Arjun, Krishna, Pooja, or Sita come from the names of important figures in Hindu mythology or practices. Indian names are not solely restricted to mythological figures or characters but can also reflect astrology attributes that would determine a prefix or starting letter of a name. Most Indians know the meaning of their name and are pleased when asked about its meaning as it shows an appreciation of the cultural naming process which is so important in Indian society.

MEN HOLDING HANDS DOESN'T MEAN THEY'RE GAY

Public displays of affection amongst couples are generally regarded as unacceptable in India. You might see a couple holding hands, but it is considered a social taboo to hug or kiss in public.

You might then be surprised to see two men holding hands or hugging in public in India, but you might also be surprised to know that it doesn't mean the men are gay. In most European nations, Canada and the US, this public display of affection of men holding hands or hugging almost certainly indicates the men are in a romantic relationship. However, in India being gay or lesbian is still considered a taboo, even though, in a landmark decision,

India's Supreme Court decriminalized homosexuality in September of 2018.

So, if you see men holding hands with each other or showing similar forms of physical intimacy, it does not mean that they are romantically involved in any way. Indians, in turn, are just as shocked to learn that in other countries this behaviour is only displayed when there is a romantic relationship between the couple.

THE INDIAN HEAD BOBBLE DECODED

The peculiar Indian head shake, wobble, or bobble is the source of much confusion and wonder amongst foreigners. It looks like a cross between a nod and a shake, often side to side, but does it mean yes? Or does it mean no? Or even maybe?

The confusion is made even worse when the bobble is silent, without a word to give any clues as to the message it's supposed to convey. However, once you discover the meaning of the head wobble and its many uses, you'll likely soon find yourself bobbling your way through many conversations yourself with this infectious gesture.

So, what is the mysterious Indian head bobble all about? In essence, the head bobble is a non-verbal gesture meaning anything from 'good' to 'I understand'.

The most common use of the head wobble is to respond in the affirmative. For example, if you ask someone if you could get some chai and they bobble their head in reply, it means 'yes'.

The head wobble is also often used as a sign that what's being said is understood. For example, if you tell someone you'd like to meet them at the office at 8:00 am and they bobble their head at you, it means that it's fine and they'll be there.

Other situations where you're likely to encounter a head bobble include:

- As an alternative to 'thank you',
  which is not commonly said in India.
- As a nonverbal alternative to 'I agree'.
- To acknowledge someone's presence.

The more vigorous the bobbling, the more understanding there is. A quick wobble means a decided 'yes' or 'alright'. A slow meandering bobble, sometimes accompanied by a smile, is a sign of friendship and respect.

Just as the various regions in India have different customs and languages, the ways in which heads are bobbled also varies. The further south you go, the more prevalent the head wobble becomes, whereas in the mountains of Northern India the gesture is less obvious. Without a doubt, however, the head wobble is the one universal gesture that unites all Indians.

JUGAARD: THE INDIAN ART OF FRUGAL INNOVATION

'Jugaad' or 'Jugaard' is a Hindi word which roughly translates as 'frugal innovation and ingenuity'. Not only are Indians ingenuous at finding innovative solutions, but they also take great pride in doing so. From a single pair of trousers with its two legs tied to an air-conditioning unit, directing the airflow to two different rooms, to unconventional business plans, seeking opportunity in adversity, doing more with less and keeping it simple, India excels in the art of jugaad.

IN INDIA, ALMOST EVERYTHING IS REVERED

There is deep respect and sacred honour in almost everything for Indians. An object or temple entrance, and even the entrance to the workplace, holds great meaning. It is not uncommon to see an Indian touch an object and then touch their forehead, then their heart, as if to say "May the object, the mind and the heart be in harmony." The same is true when an Indian enters their workplace; in this manner, the act is a silent prayer for their work to be in harmony with the mind and heart.

If an Indian finds a coin, they might pick it up and hold it to their forehead and heart to show respect to Lakshmi, the Hindu Goddess of wealth, fortune and prosperity.

PART 5

TRAVEL, HEALTH AND SAFETY

BEFORE
YOU ARRIVE

VISAS

Visitors to India can either apply for a regular visa or an e-Visa, an online application that pre-approves you for entry into India. The e-Visa is extended to passport holders of over 160 countries. These e-Visas are good for tourists, those visiting for short duration medical treatment and yoga courses, casual business visits and conferences. Previously, these required separate medical/student/business visas, but now visa categories can be combined together. However, e-Conference visas are only permitted to be combined with e-Tourist visas. The e-Visa is divided into these categories:

- e-Tourist Visa
- e-Business Visa
- e-Medical Visa
- e-Medical Attendant Visa
- e-Conference Visa

E-Visas are valid for 60 days from the date of arrival in India, except for e-Conference visas which are valid for only 30 days. Two entries are permitted on e-Tourist visas and e-Business visas, while three entries are permitted on e-Medical visas and e-Medical Attendant visas. Only one entry is permitted on e-Conference visas. The visas are non-extendable and non-convertible.

Applications for an e-Visa can be applied for a minimum of four days in advance of the date of your arrival with a window of 120 days. Example: If you are applying on 1 September, you can select an arrival date from 5 September to 2 January. Applications can be found online at the Bureau of Immigration Ministry of Home Affairs – Government of India website: indianvisaonline.gov.in/evisa.

As well as entering your travel details, you will need to upload a photograph of yourself with a white background that meets the specifications listed on the website and the photo page of your passport that shows your personal details. Your passport should have at least six months validity from the date of arrival in India. It should also have at least two blank pages for stamping by the immigration officer. Additional documents may be required depending on the type of e-Visa.

You will be required to pay the fee online with your debit or credit card. You will receive an Application ID and the Electronic Travel Authorization (ETA) will be sent to you via email within three to five days. The status of your application can be checked online. Make sure it shows 'GRANTED' before you travel.

You will need to have a copy of the ETA with you when you arrive in India and present it at the immigration counter at the airport. An immigration officer will stamp your passport with your e-Visa for entry into India.

The cost varies with each country as the visa fee depends on the nature of the reciprocal relationship between India and each country. There are four different fee amounts, ranging from zero to US$100.

You can apply for an e-Visa three times in a calendar year, between January and December.

If you have any questions regarding an e-Visa, call +91-11-24300666 or email indiatvoa@gov.in.

When applying for your e-Visa, do be aware that a number of scam commercial websites have been created to look similar to the government of India's official website, and they claim to provide online visa services to tourists. The websites do not belong to the government of India and they will charge you hefty service fees. These websites include:

- e-visaindia.com
- e-touristvisaindia.com
- indianvisaonline.org.in

BUSINESS AND EMPLOYMENT VISAS

What are the differences between a business and an employment visa, and which makes the most sense for you? First let's explore the differences.

Employment visas are issued to foreigners who are working in India for an organization registered in India. You'll need to report these earnings and are liable for taxes. Employment visas generally require you to have an offer letter from the employer stipulating your role, terms and conditions and your salary. Employment visas are usually valid for one year or the term of the contract. They can be extended in India.

Business visas are for those who would like to make a business-related trip to India to establish contacts and discuss business opportunities. This type of visa differs from an Employment visa in that the applicant won't be working for or earning an income from an organization in India. Business visa applicants may require a letter from the organization that they intend to do business with, stating the nature of the business, duration of stay, places to be visited and intention to meet expenses.

Business visas are valid for up to five or ten years, with multiple entries. However, holders usually aren't allowed to remain in India for more than 180 days at a time, unless they register with the Foreigners Regional Registration Office (FRRO).

TRAVEL VACCINES

Currently there are no vaccinations required before allowing entry into India for most foreigners, unless you've visited a country with risk of yellow fever before your arrival. However, the World Health Organization (WHO) recommends these vaccinations for travellers to India:

- Hepatitis A
- Hepatitis B
- Measles, Mumps, Rubella (MMR)
- Tetanus, Diphtheria, Pertussis (Tdap)
- Oral Polio (OPV)
- Typhoid Fever
- Varicella
- Japanese Encephalitis
- Meningococcal
- Rabies
- Yellow Fever (YF)

Immunizations are determined by several factors that you and your healthcare provider should review together, based on your health history, your travel destinations and personal choice regarding immunizations.

Some vaccinations need to be started at least four to six weeks (and up to six months) prior to your arrival into India to reach full effectiveness. You may also choose to take preventative medicine for malaria, which is a prescription medication taken before, during and after your visit.

Because health and safety requirements change over time as diseases are eliminated or new diseases start to spread, check with your healthcare provider and government websites' current recommendations before travelling to India.

ARRIVING
IN INDIA

Step number one upon arriving in India … brace yourself for impact.

Even though Delhi and Mumbai airports have earned top positions in the 'Airport Service Quality' awards by Airports Council International, the sheer number of people travelling throughout India's airports can feel utterly chaotic.[1]

One of the first signs that would indicate you are in for the beginnings of an education speaking 'Indian' is figuring out how to exit the airport. In most airports worldwide, one might look for an 'Exit' sign, but in India they use the words 'Way Out' to exit an airport. Of course, you'll be able to recognize that 'Way Out' also means 'Exit', but this might be your first experience in understanding that your familiar ways are about to be scrambled up a bit. The dictionary defines 'way out' as *"outlandish, eccentric, quirky, unusual, crazy, absurd and bizarre"*: these words accurately describe what your new and exciting adventure into India will be!

Once you step outside the airport, be prepared for a tidal wave of heat and humidity. You'll soon be engulfed by a swarm of taxi drivers vying for your business. If you have pre-arranged transportation waiting, you'll need to scan the long line of placards to find the one with your name on it. Once you see your name, the cheerful driver will greet you, as will a few enterprising friendly faces happy to carry your luggage to your vehicle, in exchange for a few rupees, which you likely don't have yet, as a small token of your appreciation. You could accept their help and offer what currency you have, or you can politely decline, but know that they will be persistent.

The heavy haze of pollution is palpable, the repugnant smells of garbage and urine in some areas is overwhelming, and the honking horns and life chatter of millions of people push the decibel levels upwards. Children with dirty faces and tattered clothes or a feeble mother holding an infant may come to your car or tug on your sleeve, raising their hand to their mouth to say they are hungry. This unnerving deluge of unfamiliar sights, sounds and smells can be exhausting, making it hard to think clearly. The sensory onslaught alone can cause even the most experienced traveller to question their typically unrattled demeanour and travel skills. For this reason, prior awareness and preparation will make your entry into India less of an assault on the body and mind.

TOUTS AND BEGGARS

Street touts and beggars are an unfortunate fact of life in India. Those begging for money – or attempting to sell something or offer services in an aggressive and persistent manner – can be intimidating, but there are proven ways to handle the situation without causing offence.

As the persistence will be inevitable, try to remain calm. Most of these people are very poor and to them you are very wealthy. Sadly, many of these people use their children to draw on the heartstrings of strangers to give more money; this only encourages this sometimes abusive behavior and often keeps children from gaining an education.

In many Western countries, people react to unwanted solicitation by replying with a firm "no", or a polite "I'll come back later"; by responding in this manner you are actually reacting and they will read this as a sign that you are interested and listening, and they'll continue the harassment. The best way to react is to simply remain silent, don't engage in any way and keep moving. This will be very difficult for many, as we don't want to come across as rude, but if you don't want to be followed endlessly, sometimes for hours, this is the best and least offensive approach. If they persist and keep following you, sometimes simply standing still and gesturing them to keep walking will help escort them along, ending the frustration for all.

GETTING
AROUND
IN INDIA

Planes, trains and automobiles are not the only way to get around India. Add to the transportation mix buses, bikes, human and auto rickshaws, farming apparatus, the occasional camels and elephants and up to five people on a single motorcycle. The rapid growth of the economy in recent years has been matched by the ever-growing demands on transportation infrastructure and services. The government is working to improve national highways and rural roads. Airports are getting upgrades and improving efficiency. Day-to-day living while navigating India's transportation and looking after yourself and your belongings will require some preplanning and additional efforts. Once you have the right information, and a willingness to ask for help, stay aware of your surroundings and maintain a good attitude, getting around India will become less intimidating, and you'll arrive from point A to point B with ease.

TRAVEL BY AIR

Getting to where you want to be in India has become easier over the past few years. India now has 20 international airports and many local airports. With the rise in private airlines, domestic air travel has become more affordable and a faster way to travel. Some airports lack the infrastructure to handle the rapid growth in travellers, so expect some occasional delays and frustrations.

TRAVEL BY ROAD

India's roads carry 90% of its travellers and 65% of its freight. While the number of roads has increased over the years, the quality has not, and many are poorly constructed or maintained. During monsoon season, flooded roads make some roads impassable, cutting off a good portion of the population. Everyday activities, appointments and meetings may be delayed or require cancellation due to impassable roads, as even on the best roads, getting from point A to point B during a downpour may create some challenges.

Driving in India is best left to the Indians. Renting a car to drive yourself is not a common practice in India but is possible in any major city. There are official rules and regulations as per the Department of Road Transport and Highways that you should be aware of, and they may or may not look a lot like the rules and regulations of your home country. Driving is on the left side of the road and drivers steer from the right side of the car. Roads are often narrow, rarely marked with a street name and are riddled with potholes, street vendors, pedestrians and cows. Painted lines on the road don't mean much, turn signals are rare and any open gap is considered fair game. The cacophony of horns honking actually means something helpful if you know their unique language.

Using taxis and smartphone apps such as 'Uber' and India-based 'Ola' are good, relatively inexpensive options for transportation. Many of the drivers speak English, but some very little and others none at all. Ride-hailing cars in India are often air-conditioned, but not always – check before you begin your trip as it might be a very uncomfortable journey if not. Nearly every Indian driver proudly adorns their vehicle. The rearview mirror, visors and dashboards are exuberantly decorated with religious affiliations such as small pictures or statues of their gods or religious symbols meant to ward off any evils. Pictures of their family or brightly coloured streamers or lights are strung along the ceiling.

Hiring drivers is not always a guarantee that they will know where it is you want to go. Be prepared with a phone number of the location so a local can guide your driver, or you might need to use your own map application to help get you to your destination. Some drivers might offer to take you to a different hotel rather than the one you have directed them to go to, or offer to take you on a tour of the city to visit a few handicraft emporiums en route to your destination. These are all choices you can of course make, but make them with caution. The hotel or handicraft emporium may be the driver's cousin, uncle, friend or brother, and the driver might get a kickback from taking you there. You might find yourself a very long distance from where you intended or you might end up on a tour lasting six hours longer than you were anticipating, seeing mostly traffic along the way.

Hiring a private car and driver is available through car hiring services. Hiring a personal driver is relatively affordable. The comfort of a nice car and chauffeur and the convenience of leaving when you like, plus local knowledge, makes travelling throughout India with a car and driver a great value for money option. While India does enjoy great train connectivity, getting train tickets and boarding trains on crowded Indian platforms can be chaotic and stressful. Hiring a private car and driver eases the worries of getting train tickets or negotiating crowded platforms. Having your own flexibility to leave anytime you wish and make as many unscheduled stops en route as you like is a true advantage.

Auto rickshaws provide an inexpensive, quick and authentic way to travel the roads of India. These doorless, three-wheel cabs ride atop a motorcycle engine and provide an up-close and personal view of the passing sights. There is even an Uber option for ordering rickshaws.

However, rickshaws provide no protection from the pollution in congested traffic, so you may want to travel with a handkerchief or light scarf to cover your nose and mouth if you are sensitive to the elements. The agility of these smaller modes of transportation often offers enough thrills to appease any adrenaline junkie.

Buses are abundant in India and a cheap way to travel. Constant stops, cramped seats, standing room only and peering, curious eyes might not be your first choice of ways to get to the office, but it can be the most authentic and enjoyable way to meet the locals, and that's something you can't put a price on.

TRAVEL BY RAILWAY

Indian Railways is Asia's largest rail system, with 121,407 kilometres (75,439 miles) of total track over a 67,368-kilometre (41,861 mile) network, with underground metros in Delhi, Kolkata, Chennai and Bengaluru. The metro system takes a bit of a learning curve to navigate but is a very popular option for both locals and visitors. On longer excursions, trains are a quick and visually appealing way to travel. India's trains offer many class options, though not all are available on every train. Comfort options include sleeper class and air-conditioned class. Some lines designate 'ladies only compartments' for female passengers.

HEALTHCARE IN INDIA

Healthcare is available in a variety of forms, including everything from an emergency room visit to a stop at the local 'medicine shop' for over-the-counter items, and some items typically only available by prescription in many countries, to the ancient wisdom of Ayurvedic practitioners.

Public hospitals in India often employ well-trained English-speaking doctors and nurses. However, a lack of equipment, funds, staff or a long wait means many locals, as well as foreigners, prefer private care whenever possible. If applicable, check with your employer to see what level of healthcare they provide to ensure adequate health insurance coverage.

TRAVEL INSURANCE

Purchasing travel insurance that covers healthcare emergencies is something to consider as well. These plans typically cover key medical benefits, providing peace of mind to international travellers, and are often provided by travel agencies as part of your airline ticket booking or through independent services such as 'World Nomads'.

Indian Railways employs more than a million people, making it the largest employer in the world.

SAFETY

India's levels of safety in any given area vary greatly just as they do in any country. Generally, foreigners will not be exposed to violent crimes, but it is wise to keep alert and be aware of your surroundings to guard against crimes such as pickpocketing, harassment of women, burglary or scams.

Entrance security checks are highly visible at public places in major cities and these often have tighter screening practices than in many other countries. Places such as shopping centres and malls, government buildings, sports venues, hotels, transportation stations and places of worship are intensely monitored. Upon entering these types of public places, it's also a common security practice for a vehicle entering a venue to be checked under the hood and in the trunk while trained security dogs sniff around the vehicle for potentially hazardous substances or harmful devices. Upon entering these sites, you will be asked to empty your pockets and place any items through security machines along with briefcases, handbags and luggage for a thorough security screening. You will then need to walk through a screening device. Security lines are separated, one for men and another for women. Men are screened by men and women are screened by women. Some places use a handheld security wand, but again men and women use separate lines. If wands are used, women are typically asked to be screened behind a curtain with a female security officer.

SAFETY
ESPECIALLY
FOR WOMEN

India does not have the best reputation for women's safety. The headlines are abundant with reports of a rape culture in India and the rampant stories of 'eve teasing', a deeply inadequate term used for sexual harassment throughout South Asia, which includes India, Pakistan, Bangladesh and Nepal. India is making progress, albeit slowly, in implementing better safety provisions for women and harsher punishments for perpetrators.

With this said, it is important for women to not be fearful of travelling to India because of safety concerns. Most female foreigners experience India without any incident. As women travel about any location, including within their own homeland, it's wise to be prepared with safety at the forefront to mitigate risk. It would be prudent for any woman's safety, in any location, to consider 'how' you travel rather than 'where' you travel.

There are a few tips to help women feel more comfortable and confident ...

As with anywhere you travel, do your research first in understanding the culture. You cannot come to India and expect to behave exactly as you do in your home country. This would be an arrogant, naïve and possibly dangerous attitude to take. In India, the genders relate differently than in other countries. You can't relate to the opposite sex in India in the same way you would in a Western country. A casual friendly word or gesture, such as a wave to say 'hello', could be perceived as an invitation for a more intimate encounter.

Because most of India is still a very traditional society, it would be wise to follow the rules of society and dress modestly. Wearing clothes that are tight fitting, low cut or show an excessive amount of skin may be perceived by some Indian men as a sign of flirtation, or worse. Wearing Indian clothing helps you to blend in a bit more, but in modern cities it may make you stand out more as many Indian women wear Western clothing. No matter how much you might try to blend in, being a foreigner is usually all it takes to be easily singled out.

Your parents may have taught you to be polite, but when travelling in India it's more important to be confident than polite. How you carry yourself plays a large part in your experience. If you hold your posture and move about in a confident way, you are less likely to attract unwanted attention. Trust your instincts. If you feel that someone is a potential threat or is harassing you, walk away immediately.

If you are in trouble, don't be afraid to call out for help. Make a scene and be loud about it. Social shaming plays a big role in Indian society, and the chances are good that 'aunties' and 'uncles' (older members of Indian society) will crowd around and defend you. You could also solicit the help of an Indian male travelling with his wife or children.

If a male teenager or man wants to take a picture with you, understand that two things are possible: 1) A queue will form and you'll feel like a celebrity momentarily, but this gets old very quickly; 2) They aren't always taking these photos in an innocent way. Often times, especially teenage boys will ask to take a photo, only to show your photo to anyone who will look and tell the story of your scandalous night together or photoshop it and potentially compromise you on the internet. If a male asks for a photo, say that you will only take a group photo or simply decline.

Lastly, it's important to be aware and knowledgeable of what's happening in the news, but don't let that taint your perception of Indian men. As in any country, there are good, upstanding men and there are those who prey on women. Be careful, but don't place all men into the latter category.

EMERGENCY CONTACTS

To reach the immediate services of the police, ambulance, and the fire department, dial 112 where an operator will direct the call to the appropriate department for immediate help.

Your government's official website will have information about how to contact your country's embassy in India should you need assistance. Many countries also provide free services to their citizens and nationals travelling and living abroad to enroll their trip with the nearest embassy or consulate, such as the US Smart Traveler Enrollment Program (STEP). Services such as STEP provide important information from the embassy regarding safety conditions in your destination country, helping you to make informed decisions about your travel plans. They also help the embassy contact you in case of an emergency, whether natural disaster, civil unrest or family emergency.

The three colours of the
Indian national flag are saffron
(for courage and sacrifice),
white (for purity and the path to
righteousness) and green (for
India's connection to the Earth).
The 24-spoke wheel in the centre
represents progress and is the
depiction of the Ashoka Chakra,
a Buddhist symbol.

PART 6

TOP TRAVEL DESTINATIONS AND ATTRACTIONS

India's tourism is booming! Over 10 million foreign tourists traveled to India in 2018 and the numbers are rising each year. India is expected to establish itself as the third-largest travel and tourism economy by 2028 in terms of GDP, according to a 2018 economic impact report by the World Travel & Tourism Council (WTTC).[1, 2, 3]

The WTTC report also said India will add nearly 10 million jobs in the tourism sector by 2028 and that the total number of jobs dependent directly or indirectly on the travel and tourism industry will increase from 42.9 million in 2018 to 52.3 million in 2028. This would make India the seventh-largest travel and tourism economy in the world.

India is certainly an exotic land of magnificent mystery and intrigue, drawing people to it from all parts of the globe. There's a plethora of cultural treasures and stunning natural attractions in India, making it impossible to list them all. Here is just a 'tip of the iceberg' collection of extraordinary landmarks and natural beauty sites, listed by region.

NORTH

OLD AND NEW DELHI are a 'must see', showcasing the diversity of life and culture India encompasses. Historically rich and culturally significant. *Best time to visit: October to March.*

AGRA is home to the Taj Mahal, one of the Seven Wonders of the World. Tourists from around the world visit India just to witness this spectacular monument. This majestic story of love is the cultural epitome of India. *Best time to visit: April to October.*

NAINITAL is one of the many beautiful hill cities. Hike to the Himalayas, visit the Sri Aurobindo Ashram or visit Jim Corbett National Park where you might spot a Bengal tiger or a wild elephant. *Best time to visit: Summer is best for tiger sightings, November to February for other activities.*

SRINAGAR is the Gem of Kashmir and known for its enthralling natural beauty. Also called 'Heaven on Earth', this captivating place does not disappoint. *Best time to visit: April to October.*

RISHIKESH is the birthplace of yoga and a popular place to come to meditate. Striking a perfect balance of peace and nature, adventure awaits with a fierce and fast ride along the rapids of the Ganges River. *Best time to visit: September to November and February to June.*

SHIMLA is the queen of the northern hills. Explore this scenic and most famous hill city with a toy train ride from Kalka to Shimla, making its way through the pine forests and lush valleys. *Best time to visit: March to June.*

MATHURA is said to be the birthplace of Lord Krishna. Along the serene banks of the Yamuna river, this 'city of gods' offers peace and is a place for contemplation on Lord Krishna's various philosophies of love. *Best time to visit: November to March.*

AMRITSAR is deeply rooted in history, culture, food and religion. The daily sunset 'lowering of the flag' ceremony on the borders of Pakistan and India is witnessed by hundreds of people every day on both sides. To experience the extraordinary gilded, Golden Temple is time well spent and not easily forgotten. *Best time to visit: November to February.*

KHAJURAHO is where you'll find the largest group of Hindu and Jain temples in the world. This UNESCO World Heritage Site has awed generations with its intricate carvings and, most famously, the erotic sculptures. *Best time to visit: October to February.*

MANALI is India's honeymoon capital. This lover's paradise has a fairy tale presence with lush green forests, sprawling meadows, gushing blue streams and a lingering scent of pine in the air. Plenty of upscale streets, river adventures and trekking trails. *Best time to visit: October to June.*

It took over 22,000 builders from India, Persia, Europe and the Ottoman Empire, along with some 1,000 elephants, to build the Taj Mahal. The Taj Mahal is an enormous mausoleum commissioned in 1632 by the Mughal emperor Shah Jahan to house the remains of his beloved wife, Mumtaz Mahal.

NORTHWEST

JAIPUR is the capital of India's Rajasthan and evokes the royal family who once ruled the region. Also called the 'Pink City' for its trademark architectural colour, its opulence stands ever royal, with its City Palace complex, complete with gardens, courtyards and museums. *Best time to visit: October to March.*

UDAIPUR is called the 'Venice of the East' and shines with some of the most gracious luxury heritage hotels and floating palaces, but it will embrace you warmly with its grandeur at any budget. *Best time to visit: September to March.*

JODHPUR, complete with cobbled pavements and echoing of an ancient Rajasthan, is a mesmerizing landscape of azure homes. *Best time to visit: October to February.*

JAISALMER is the place to go for the best desert experience. Indulge in some exciting adventures such as dune bashing, a camel safari and desert camping. *Best time to visit: October to February.*

NORTHEAST

VARANASI is one of the world's oldest cities and the spiritual capital of India. Millions of pilgrims travel to this holy Hindu city located on the Ganges River each month to offer prayers and perform rituals. A sunrise boat ride along the banks reveals the beauty of this sacred city. *Best time to visit: October to February.*

SARNATH is the birthplace of Buddhism, marking the spot where Buddha delivered his first sermon. *Best time to visit: October to February.*

ASSAM is home to Kaziranga National Park, which has the largest number of Indian rhinos and where the Elephant Festival is hosted. *Best time to visit: October to April.*

SIKKIM shares a border with Bhutan, Tibet and Nepal and is home to a host of ancient Buddhist monasteries. Glaciers, alpine meadows and wildflowers grace the dramatic landscape which includes Kangchenjunga, India's highest mountain. *Best time to visit: March to June and September to December.*

EAST

KOLKATA is where you can visit the home of Mother Teresa and her Missionaries of Charity. This is a city with a perfect balance of old-world Bengali charm and modern culture. *Best time to visit: November to February.*

 DARJEELING is where you can catch the steam-powered 'toy train' with the Darjeeling Himalayan Railway to Siliguri while enjoying the rolling hills and lush green tea plantations with views of the Himalayas. *Best time to visit: February to March and September to December.*

SOUTH

KOCHI *(Cochin)*, located in the tropical southwestern state of Kerala, was named one of the ten paradises of the world by *National Geographic Traveler.* To witness the Chinese fishing nets against a spectacular Indian evening horizon is truly unforgettable. *Best time to visit: October to February.*[4]

MADURAI epitomizes South Indian Hindu architecture with its Sri Meenakshi and Sundareswarar temples. *Best time to visit: October to March.*

KANYAKUMARI or **CAPE COMORIN** is the southernmost tip of the Indian peninsula, where the Bay of Bengal, the Arabian Sea and the Indian Ocean meet. *Best time to visit: October to February.*

THE ANDAMAN ISLANDS are a water lover's paradise off the southeast shores of India in the Bay of Bengal. From perfect sunsets to the thrills of scuba diving, these islands have it all. *Best time to visit: November to May.*

MYSURU *(Mysore)* is the perfect combination of the old and new. The city, which has royal status, is a rising

IT hub and is renowned around the world for its gorgeous silk sarees, sweet treats and sandalwood. *Best time to visit: Throughout the year, but October to March is the most pleasant.*

MAMALLAPURAM *(Mahabalipuram)* is the epitome of art and architecture. This quaint little town famous for its monuments and temples that date back to the seventh century is a living witness to the great works of the Pallava dynasty. Krishna's Butter Ball, an enormous, precariously balanced boulder perched on a steep rock slope, is said to be a huge dollop of stolen butter dropped by the gods. *Best time to visit: November to February.*

PUDUCHERRY *(Pondicherry)* is a quaint, little beach town entrenched with French colonial heritage. Famed to be the French Riviera of the East, Pondicherry or Puducherry is a favourite tourist spot. The delicious seafood and delectable French bakeries are a must. *Best time to visit: October to March.*

COORG is widely known for being the 'Scotland of the South', an enchanting hill city with views of mystic airy clouds blending with the greenery of the hills. Have you ever tried waterfall rappelling? If not, this is the place to do it! *Best time to visit: Coorg is a year-round destination. October to March is best for adventure activities.*

SOUTHWEST

HAMPI holds the ancient chronicles left by Persian and European travellers at this UNESCO World Heritage Site. Giant boulders precariously perched dotting the landscape have captivated travellers for centuries. *Best time to visit: October to February.*

GOA has the best-known beaches in India and is also home to many wildlife sanctuaries. Bike expeditions and exploring the rugged terrain of the forest and the magical Dudhsagar Falls are also popular. *Best time to visit: November to February.*

MUMBAI is the gem on the shore of the Arabian Sea. This carefree city that never sleeps is about its people, the spirit of enjoying life and Bollywood. *Best time to visit: November to February.*

The official currency of India is the Indian rupee.
The currency symbol is ₹ and the code is INR.

Indian rupees are not available for purchase
outside of India. ATMs in India are a great way
to avoid the exchange centres and elevated
rates to get Indian rupees directly.

India's International Dialling Code is +91.

The Time Zone is India Standard Time (IST).

The 12-hour notation is widely used in daily life.

India does not follow daylight saving time.

The date format India uses is DD-MM-YYYY.

PART 7

BUSINESS ETIQUETTE AND PROTOCOL

BUSINESS HIERARCHIES

India maintains a level of caste/hierarchy in its business structure, especially amongst its leaders and employees. India is still working through its caste system reforms, and in most of the big cities large corporations tend to run their businesses closer to the Western style. However, the employee/employer relationship continues to be traditional in that the employees even at the mid-management or senior management levels cannot make any final decisions until the head of the company/executive manager agrees.

There is also variation of hierarchy styles in the North versus the South of India. In the North, the style of management tends to be more open and progressive. Cities like Delhi often have a startup hub environment that feels international in nature. Whereas in the South, in cities such as Chennai, Hyderabad and Bangalore, the tone changes to a much stricter one with an accountable hierarchy within the company.

THINGS TO CONSIDER WHEN DOING BUSINESS IN INDIA

- Indian business culture tends to function in a similar way to the country's family structures, with particular regard to the boundaries of employer/employee relationships.
- Employees respect their company's organization chart and, more often than not, follow it rather than try to go above their boss's head.
- Most companies have a managing director and often the top manager reports to (or is that) individual. Ultimately the managing director makes all the final decisions. However, if you're dealing with an international company, it will usually have a managing director but may still need approval from leadership in another country.
- When working with companies in India, keep in mind that you must provide all the details of a project or request. If you are working on a contract or looking to do business, always meet with the top manager.

- Fishing for information from managers and employees on the lower part of the totem pole will be looked upon as being disrespectful and may raise red flags. It may also reduce your chances of doing business.
- When you meet with senior female managers in government and education roles, they will often wear a saree. This is also the case when senior female managers give talks or lectures. In North India, dressing for women is far more progressive, while in the south you still see a large number of women wearing sarees and traditional clothing to work. The saree can be seen as a sign of power and respect and is considered a celebration of the Indian woman. Recently, it's been gaining popularity amongst young Indian women who want to embrace their local heritage.

GREETINGS

Greetings in India are usually very simple and Western, such as a handshake between contemporaries. Handshakes are more common in big cities and within large enterprises. When dealing with older adults or traditional organizations, which include government bodies, you can bring your two hands together to give respect. You may want to also say "Namaste", but this isn't always required, unless dealing with a more traditional segment of society. As India is still becoming accustomed to women in business, most men find it awkward to shake hands with a woman, particularly in the south. If you find yourself in this scenario, just bring your hands together to show a respectful hello.

You really have to feel the tone of the meeting and the people you are dealing with, and there will be variations between the North and South. South India tends to be more conservative in nature, while the North is more progressive.

Below are some tips on business etiquette and style:

- **BUSINESS CARDS**: Carry a business card when going to meetings as it's still very much a part of the business culture. However, new technology and awareness of the environment have also led to e-cards being used. When receiving a business card, put it away respectfully.
- **MEETINGS**: Make sure to confirm your meeting by email, with time and address.
- **WHEN IN PERSON**: Give yourself ample time to arrive at your meeting as traffic in India can cause significant delays. While India was once known for 'India Time' jokes, it's no longer the case. Indians respect punctuality and want to do business with people who respect time as well.
- **VIRTUAL MEETINGS**: To save time, you may want to have a few virtual meetings via Skype, Duo or Google Hangouts. Again, the protocol is to confirm via email and supply the links and details to the virtual meeting.
- **EMAIL PROTOCOL**: Always start your emails with Mr or Mrs and/or Sir or Madam. Unless otherwise told by the person, do not refer to them by first name

basis and keep the email short and concise. Be sure to track everything on email to help you clarify any misunderstandings that may occur due to miscommunication.

- **FORMAL COMMUNICATION:**
  - › Verbal communication – always greet professionals and individuals with respect by using Mr/Mrs and/or Sir or Madam.
  - › Remain calm and reconfirm any agreement or information that's been shared, especially if in doubt. This is important as you may face misunderstandings due to varying degrees of English competency.
  - › Non-verbal communication – be polite, don't stare, handshake with right hand as left hand is considered offensive, and bow when using the salutation "Namaste".
- **BUSINESS STYLE:** Western wear is prevalent and standard for offices and meetings. For men this means a white shirt, trousers and jacket, and for ladies this means a simple top or blouse paired with trousers. While in some areas you will find some women wearing traditional sarees, it's no longer the norm.

DECISION-MAKING STYLES AND BUSINESS NEGOTIATIONS

Any decision for a business will always be made by the highest-ranking official in the office and/or the managing director or owner. Be sure to understand a company's organizational chart from the beginning, so as to not get stuck in a situation where you are dealing with the wrong person. Remember, no matter what, the boss is the boss and is ultimately the person signing the contract.

When you're negotiating during October-November keep in mind that some companies and business owners will wait for Diwali to sign the contract; it is considered a special and auspicious time. This is a time to rejoice and will help you to forge alliances.

CHARACTERISTICS OF EMPLOYERS

Most companies are still family-owned, with the larger companies being held by what are known as 'promoters'. These companies run the same as any Fortune 500 company and follow Western-style protocols. Smaller to medium-sized enterprises tend to take on the characteristics and culture of the owners, offering a more intimate relationship and less corporate structure.

CHARACTERISTICS OF EMPLOYEES

For retaining and hiring employers, you will need to offer competitive packages and salary incentives. Indians value their families, so employees look for companies that can offer a work-life balance, allowing them to still enjoy family time.

FOOD AND DRINK, GIFTS AND ENTERTAINMENT

A vegetarian diet is the standard in India; however, while in the south, food served at business gatherings tends to be predominantly vegetarian, in the north, meals often include meat dishes.

You may find yourself invited to weddings, especially around the months of Diwali, or what is known as 'Wedding Season'. Attending a wedding is a sign of respect to the bride and groom, as well as to the person who invited you. But be careful not to overdo the gifts as this may be looked upon as a bribe.

When invited into the home of an associate, be mindful of removing your shoes, as this custom is still often followed. With regard to alcohol, the serving of liquor during employee/employer entertainment is prevalent in the north, while in the south it is not.

INTERNATIONAL RELATIONS

India has made huge strides in the last decade, embracing technology and leading in global development. It is quickly emerging as one the fastest-developing nations in Asia. While China leads in population, India leads in democracy and development, and enjoys a worldwide reputation as a nation that proactively improves the lives of its citizens.

A lot of the improvement happening in India has been due to its strong political ties with strategic nations and maintaining a rather neutral relationship with most of the world, as well as promoting policies that ensure the growth of its educated workforce.

TIME ON THE GROUND

The world sees India as a friend and as a country full of opportunities, however difficult it can be to figure out as a nation. You'll need to spend at least two years in India to begin to develop a sense of 'figuring it out'. We recommend that anyone looking to explore India as a market opportunity should first visit the country and get to know it and its people. Unless you're a large enterprise ready to take on the market through smart acquisitions, the only way to enter and penetrate this market is to live, breathe and explore it from the ground up. So, while the world views India as a land of spiritual growth, teas, curry and spicy foods, as an entrepreneur you must see it as your next home! Only then can you create and profit.

HOW THEY WORK WITH FOREIGNERS AT HOME

Indians are often friendly and open to working with foreigners, so do join local Facebook groups and visit local networking organizations to build connections. Be prepared to have lots of 'chai' (tea) and 'chaat' (snacks), even in your office environment. Indians love their breaks and time to connect with fellow business partners, so be ready to embrace the warm and welcoming atmosphere.

THINGS WE CAN THANK INDIA FOR

Chess originated in India in
the 6th century AD when it was
called 'Chaturanga'.

Yoga originated in India over
5,000 years ago.

Calculus, trigonometry and algebra
all originated in India.

The first mining of diamonds was
done in India in approximately
4th century BC.

The extraction and purifying
techniques required to make sugar
were first developed in India.

PART 8

STARTING YOUR BUSINESS IN INDIA

MARKET ENTRY STRUCTURES AND STRATEGIES

This section has been designed to provide you with quick tips to help you understand what parts of India interest you in terms of market entry and what are the simple processes that you will have to take to 'officially' launch your business in India.

SOME SIMPLE TIPS FOR ENTRY AND STRATEGIES ARE AS FOLLOWS

- Take time to learn the market. In the latter part of this book we help you understand the various states welcoming foreigners who want to do business in India.
- Visit as many times as possible before launching. Taking six months to explore before going for long-term business visas will help you understand if you want to dedicate the five years it may take to get your business going in India.
- Patience is key. Many foreigners leave soon after due to the stress of local processes.
- Learn from and connect with your local country government offices to help you understand the marketplace and opportunities.
- Look for the right partners locally who can help you.
- Knowledge and relationships are key.

MARKET OPPORTUNITIES

If you are going to start a business in India, here are some segments of the economy where you may find opportunities. There are startup incubators and groups for each of these segments, and you can network to learn more via organizations like the PHD Chamber of Commerce and The Confederation of Indian Industry (CII).

- Education
- Healthcare
- Energy
- Food and Agriculture
- Health and Wellness

Using technologies such as blockchain, artificial intelligence, virtual reality and augmented reality are welcomed in the above industries.

Companies and entrepreneurs that can prove they are creating jobs for the local economy have an advantage. Currently India is on track to need on average over

8.2 million new jobs per year to keep unemployment at a minimum.[1] While big businesses create jobs, the government understands that the growth and influx of jobs will come from small- to medium-sized business owners, and they are willing to offer incentives from a state level to support this. So, start thinking of how to innovate in a country where your solution could have a global impact.

If the state of Uttar Pradesh were a country it would be ranked the fifth largest as it has over 200 million residents.[2]

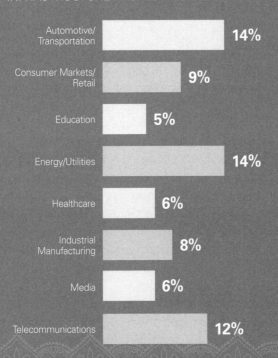

TOP 7 INDIA GROWTH INDUSTRIES

BASED ON THE IMPROVEMENT OF TECHNOLOGY INFRASTRUCTURE AND NETWORKS

Automotive/Transportation **14%**

Consumer Markets/Retail **9%**

Education **5%**

Energy/Utilities **14%**

Healthcare **6%**

Industrial Manufacturing **8%**

Media **6%**

Telecommunications **12%**

The above is based on a global average ranked against the US, China, Japan and the UK. It's also based on KPMG's innovation lab's finding from Dec 2017.

BUSINESS WISDOM

As a country of 1.3 billion people, India offers tremendous opportunities. With 67% of the population living in rural India, the government is working closely with its private sector companies to ensure infrastructure continues to improve in rural parts of India, specifically in the mobile technology field to also ensure the growth of 'smart villages' and to help improve village lifestyles. Entrepreneurs are being asked to come up with smart village concepts and to innovate for rural consumers who often don't own mobile devices. With urban cities expected to have a population of 600 million people by 2030, the migration from rural settings into the larger urban cities is expected to increase opportunities across various sectors such as automotive, retail and technology.[1]

In doing business in India, you must keep in mind that business style may vary based on region. This book shares the standard for business across India, but we recommend you always do research if you are going to explore more rural parts of India.

SUPPORT FOR BUSINESS

The Indian government has made it its mission, with initiatives such as Invest India, to make it easy for foreigners to enter the market. Each region has a dedicated group and website where you can find details on doing business in places such as Chennai, Punjab, Gujarat, etc. India's recent efforts have moved it up in the world ranking of countries for ease of doing business to 77th place in 2018/2019.

Below are some helpful resources for foreign investors and entrepreneurs to review in order to make doing business in India easier, including information on useful government programmes.

- **INVEST INDIA WEBSITE** - The primary government initiative to partner with when looking to enter the market.
- **MAKE IN INDIA WEBSITE** - Provides information on new policies and the fastest-growing areas to invest in.

LEGAL AND REGULATORY FRAMEWORK

FOR FOREIGN INVESTORS AND ENTREPRENEURS

We recommend that before making any final decisions, you consult a local attorney or accountant. The Invest India website and Startup India's website have a lot of information on what's needed to incorporate.[1] With the advent of a digital India, the processes required for starting a business have improved and it can be done in as little as two weeks.

Most individuals are recommended to incorporate as a standalone private limited company, while it's recommended that owners of existing businesses are recommended to create subsidiaries.

Here is what you need to know:

To set up a stand-alone private limited company, you will need to make sure you have a local director and local address to file the paperwork. It will be considered a new company with shares held by the foreign director and the local director.

1. A subsidiary company/wholly owned subsidiary also requires an Indian director and a registered office address. It will be considered a branch of the parent company, where:

   a. 100% Foreign Direct Investment (FDI) is allowed through automatic route

   b. Limited share where foreign national directors/shareholders own 99.99%

   c. Indian director owns 0.01% required, as per Ministry of Corporate Affairs (MCA)

   d. FDI is part of the registration. No approvals are required for transactions between companies.

2. Timeframe to incorporate:

   a. Fourteen to 20 business days to incorporate and get approvals

   b. Funds must be deposited from your foreign accounts to begin banking in both types of incorporations.

FEES INVOLVED TO INCORPORATE

These are estimates based on the authors' experiences and are expressed in US dollars. These rates may be lower if you are doing a lot of the paperwork yourself and via government websites such as Startup India.

Basics may include, but are not limited to, the following documents to register a business in India:

- **DIN:** Director Identification Number
  › Anyone wanting to do business and be a director in India requires a DIN. This number is used to track all the companies you are involved in and used for taxation as well.
- **DSC:** Digital Signature Certificate
- **PAN:** Personal Account Number
  › This is required to carry out any form of financial transaction including opening up your bank accounts, and is used in tax reporting.
- **GST:** Goods and Services Tax
  › The GST has to be applied for in order to collect and charge taxes on your goods or services when invoicing your clients.
- **NAME APPROVALS:** checking availability of your proposed business name.

- **CERTIFICATES OF SHARES:** printed/e-certificates
- **ANNUAL TAX FILING**
- **AUDITOR APPOINTMENT**
- **APOSTILLE DOCUMENTS:** Passports, birth certificates, and any official government document being used must have an apostille certification. This service and cost varies between countries; check with your local embassy before travelling. This will help speed up your incorporation.

Fees for all of the above, if you have an attorney or chartered accountant, are likely to be above $1,500, but some companies charge $3,000 or more. The fees, which vary between cities and states, can be seen as an investment in freeing yourself up from the task. You can do it all yourself, but it will take longer.

Documents required to register as an Indian director:

1. **PAN** (Permanent Account Number) card (mandatory for Indian Citizens)
2. **PROOF OF ADDRESS** (e.g. voter's ID/ driving license/Aadhar card/ passport)
3. The DSC application has to have affixed to it a signed **PASSPORT-SIZE PHOTO**
4. **MOBILE NUMBER** and **EMAIL ADDRESS** should be included in Section 3 of the DSC application with a signed declaration, and should have attached the PAN card and proof of address with a self-attested signature and the proofs signed by any gazetted officer.

KEY ORGANIZATIONS/ BODIES TO ASSIST INTERNATIONAL BUSINESS

India can feel intimidating, especially for a foreigner who is doing business or working there. Here are a few key organizations to help you get through the process and find partners and networks to help you as you learn more about the market and its people.

- **INVEST INDIA**: updates on FDI and policy
- **MAKE IN INDIA**: information on incorporating and local opportunities
- **SHEROES**: ideal for female entrepreneurs to build networks
- **INTERNATIONS**: network with local expats
- **NITI AAYOG**: National Institution for Transforming India, Government of India – government think tank, open to meeting and hearing ideas and solutions

- **STARTUP IN INDIA**
- **PHD CHAMBER:** Based out of Delhi, this organization often holds meetings and can help in incorporating, applying for financing and finding local mentors to work with
- **WOMEN ENTREPRENEURSHIP PLATFORM** (WEP). Officially launched in 2019, the platform was spearheaded by Niti Aayog and is open to women entrepreneurs from overseas to join and participate alongside their female Indian counterparts. The programme is also open to having female entrepreneurs from overseas to mentor. It's a great platform to engage with and understand more of the opportunities women entrepreneurs have in the region.

STARTUP HUBS AND INCUBATORS

- **TIE** (This Indus Entrepreneur) Global is a Silicon Valley-based NGO whose mission is to offer mentorship, support and nurturing to startups. The group was started by a group of individuals whose roots were in India, and it currently has various chapters throughout the country. The group also offers networking and seed funding opportunities.
- **NEXUS STARTUP HUB AT THE AMERICAN CENTER:** US Embassy collaboration in Delhi.
- **THE CARTIER WOMEN INITIATIVE** is not limited to India. It is a global initiative to recognize female entrepreneurs and offer them a financial prize to help them grow.
- **THE US DEPARTMENT OF STATE, GLOBAL ENTREPRENEURSHIP SUMMITS:** Another great programme with global exposure, allowing entrepreneurs from all over the world to connect and grow globally. This is an annual event that can help foster global relationships with fellow entrepreneurs.
- **THE BRITISH COUNCIL IN INDIA:** A great resource for UK citizens to connect and learn more about opportunities in India.

FDI RESTRICTIONS TO CONSIDER

Foreign Direct Investments (FDI) incentives have been aggressive over the last ten years to promote and attract foreign investors and nurture growth.[1] However, as recently as December 2018, new restrictions have been put in place for online e-commerce companies such as Amazon, Flipkart and Walmart, the last of which is looking to enter the market in 2019/2020 via its Flipkart acquisition.

The major restriction coming into effect in 2019, which will affect e-commerce retail brands, includes the following stipulation:[2]

> *An entity having equity participation by e-commerce marketplace entity or its group companies or having control on its inventory by e-commerce marketplace entity or its group companies, will not be permitted to sell its products on the platform run by such marketplace entity.*

Ultimately what this means is that companies can only sell their products on their own online websites. This is a cause for concern because many of the brands being sold on e-commerce sites, such as Myntra, Amazon, Flipkart, Jabong and Nykaa, have been selling into the Indian consumer market for years. They have disrupted the market so much that smaller vendors have been impacted and have pushed the government to re-evaluate its system to allow for fair competition.

Many of the major brands such as Nike, Reebok, Aldo, Kenneth Cole, Levy's, etc. have entered the country via joint venture partnerships and distributors or by franchising and licensing out their names. This method of entering the country as a brand via joint venture may continue to be the most effective way for Western brands to get a foothold in the market as these new regulations emerge to help the small business owner brands grow. These new restrictions may not affect foreign small business owners and entrepreneurs as much as they will big businesses, and thereby may actually help those of you who are looking to enter the Indian market as a new brand.

To learn about the latest FDI Regulation changes, check the Invest India and Make in India websites.

TAXATION AND GOVERNMENT INCENTIVES

Once you have incorporated and are clear on the type of product or service you will be offering, your accountant will apply for the appropriate GST ID that needs to be registered with the local taxation authorities and used when filing your business taxes.

GST is a country-wide taxation reform initiative by the Modi administration to make it easier for states to tax goods. It sought to remove the multiple taxes which previously existed and have just one tax across the board for individual products or services. This has made it easier for business, but there has been an increase in the pricing of goods and services. Previously the product pricing printed was the price inclusive of tax. However, while GST was transitioning, you saw the price on the package remained the same, but the tax was added after. Local consumers felt that GST allowed companies to increase their product pricing.

GST also brought to light the service tax in restaurants. This received mixed responses because overall most people don't leave a tip in India. However, some restaurants do add a service tax which is supposed to be a pool shared with the servers of the business.

Taxation as it pertains to LLPs (limited liability partnerships) and subsidiaries:[1]

- LLPs pay 30% of their global income
- LLPs must file annual returns
- when LLPs distribute profits, this is not taxable to the partners
- repatriation of capital contributions to LLPs
- subsidiaries profits repatriation by way of dividends subject to Dividend Distribution Tax (DDT) in the hands of the company at the rate of 20.36%.

Taxation as it pertains to liaison offices:

- not subject to tax as they do not conduct business activities
- they have to obtain a PAN and TAN (tax deduction and collection account number)
- they must also file annual statements.

Taxation for project offices/branch offices:

- looked upon as a permanent establishment in India
- taxable at 40%
- requires PAN/TAN
- repatriation at the time of closure
- not subject to additional taxes.

STARTUP TAX INCENTIVES

The government has taken initiatives to reduce taxes on new startups in business for five years or less, and offers them a three-year tax holiday on 100% of their profits.

Agreements to help owners of businesses avoid having their employees double taxed have come into effect, and the government has created bilateral agreements with different countries to protect you as a business owner who may be hiring overseas employees to come into the region.

Here are two points that you need to know about:

- **DOUBLE TAXATION AVOIDANCE AGREEMENT (DTAA):** This agreement takes place between India and your home country so that you are not double taxed in the source country as well as your resident country. Based on your resident country, do research this more as each country has a different process.

- **SOCIAL SECURITY:** Like most countries, India has a system in place for social security for its citizens, and employees are required to make contributions towards the fund. To protect foreign employees, India has entered into the Social Security Agreement (SSA) and what is referred to as the Bilateral Comprehensive Economic Agreements (BCEA) with different countries. You must check with your respective countries and human resources departments when setting up an office in India to obtain a 'Certificate of Coverage' to claim exemption from Indian social security.

MANAGING MONEY

When doing business in India, you will need an accountant. They will help you set up the business accounts and personal accounts that you can use while in India. However, you can continue to use your international bank's ATM/cash point, credit cards and checks if and when you need to make payments.

IN ORDER TO OPEN A BANK ACCOUNT IN INDIA YOU WILL NEED THE FOLLOWING:

- local address and local phone number
- PAN card
- resident certificate (obtained from the local police station once you have registered with your local Foreign Regional Registration Office (FRRO)).

If you are of Indian descent, you have access to opening a non-resident ordinary Rupee (NRO) account, allowing you to transact between your Indian bank account and your overseas bank with ease. The option is widely used.

Do note that the government is becoming more and more strict with banking and managing money. This is due to the increase of digital banking and to reduce corruption and the possible influx of 'black' money.

NATIONAL SYMBOLS
OF INDIA

The lotus flower is the national
flower of India.

India's national bird is the peacock.

The Bengal tiger is the national
animal of India.

The mango is the national
fruit of India.

The banyan tree is the national
tree of India.

Cricket is India's national sport.

PART 9

THINGS TO CONSIDER WHEN DOING BUSINESS IN INDIA

In this section we cover everything from hiring employees, attracting customers in digital India, setting the right price for your products and services, and considering intellectual property risks and strategies.

HIRING AND BUILDING A TEAM

You'll need to know what to look out for when hiring a team in India and what sort of qualifications to expect.

India's university system is wide-ranging and some of the top institutes are of high quality. Below is a quick guide to some of the top universities within different sectors as well as the degrees they provide.

ENGINEERING

The Bachelor of Technology (B.Tech) is an undergraduate professional engineering degree. This is amongst the most widely sought-after qualifications in India. It leads to specializations like chemical, mechanical and software engineering. The most reputable colleges are the Indian Institutes of Technology, Birla Institute of Technology Pilani, and the National Institute of Technology.

MEDICINE

In India, medicine is pursued after high school with a combined Bachelor of Medicine and Bachelor of Surgery (MBBS) degree. The All India Institute of Medical Sciences, New Delhi is the most reputable institute for medicine.

LAW

Some students pursue law after high school with a five-year long Bachelor of Law degree from institutes such as the National Law School of India University, Bangalore and NALSAR Hyderabad. Others choose to pursue a three-year course after their graduation from university.

FASHION AND ART SCHOOLS

India has two top fashion colleges whose graduates are amongst some of the most talented in the industry. These colleges are often open to partnerships with retailers and fashion brands who want to hire their students or offer them internships. While traditional degrees such as medicine and law have been the norm in India, non-traditional hotelier, fashion and art degrees are amongst some of the fastest growing in terms of talent pools. The most reputable colleges for degrees in fashion are NIFT (National Institute of Fashion Technology), which is a government school and whose students are from diverse backgrounds, and Pearl Academy, a private institution, where the teaching style allows the students to grow, explore and innovate. Most students who graduate from Pearl Academy have to present business plans and samples of work to show full mastery. The school is also building a strong journalism and photography programme with a faculty of international teachers from Europe and the US.

OTHER GRADUATE/ UNDERGRADUATE DEGREES

Typically, undergraduate degrees in all other major fields are pursued at institutes like Delhi University or the University of Mumbai. These are typically Bachelor of Arts or Science programmes.

To get to know more about the quality of your prospective employee's education, you can take a look at the national rankings published by *India Today* annually. Even if you don't recognize the name of the college or university, don't worry. India has a large network of public and private, central and state universities. The thing to ensure is that the university is affiliated with the University Grants Commission (UGC), which is the government body regulating funding and quality of all public and many good quality private institutes in India. A quick search on the university should instantly reveal this.

Generally, public universities in India are well-established. With private universities, you should dig deeper to ensure that it is a good quality institute.

SPEAKING ENGLISH

Almost all good quality institutes of India are English-medium and their graduates should have excellent proficiency in the language. However, since the ability to speak English fluently is often shaped by childhood exposure to the language, some highly educated individuals might struggle with it. Therefore, if the position you are hiring for requires an excellent command of English, it is a good idea to have a phone conversation with prospective employees before shortlisting them. You should be able to find a candidate pretty quickly because India has a huge population (125 million and growing) of individuals proficient in the language.

SEARCHING FOR THE PERFECT CANDIDATE

While websites like naukri.com and monster.com are popular amongst job hunters, LinkedIn remains the top choice for startups. You might also find some good people to work with at startup meetings and summits.

DEMONETIZATION AND DIGITAL INDIA

On 8 November 2016, in an effort to reduce and combat corruption, the government accomplished two major things regarding demonetization. First, they removed the old 500 and 1,000 rupee notes from circulation, adding new 500 and 2,000 notes. They set restrictions as to how much can be deposited without a tax fee or penalty. This meant that everyone who held more than two lakhs in cash, or roughly $3,000, would now have to report earnings and/or open a bank account.

The country was able to aggressively turn traditional users of money into digital users overnight. In addition, the rural user now needed to go to a nearby city or state to open an account to learn the new banking and finance laws. For those in villages, this was actually an empowering and liberating experience. For some, this was the first time a member of their family had opened an account, linking them to a system that also introduces them to credit and the ability to receive government subsidies instantly to their accounts.

Suddenly the use of digital wallets and online payments became possible and the country was embracing it, with its citizens in 'Tier 3 cities' (see chart) and beyond becoming connected to technology.

The second major thing this did was bring 'Digital India' to life. The programme to digitize its government systems. The Aadhar programme for digital identification and digital signatures was entering the mainstream and was no longer limited to the upper class. This process of demonetization took away the fear that many had about completing transactions online or via their mobile devices.

Today Indians everywhere, from cities to villages, are transacting via digital wallets, using their mobile devices to make payments, send money to family members and make purchases online. Mapping is also easier, allowing public and private sector companies to develop and create for the people in areas in which they once had no access to information.

FINDING CUSTOMERS IN INDIA

To reach the digital consumer in India, you need to address local needs and have the solutions available online. As entrepreneurs and small- to medium-sized business owners, you have an opportunity to take advantage of this digital phenomenon by working with smaller companies and forging relationships directly within the areas you can address.

One of the biggest opportunities in India lies in the online e-commerce segment. Companies such as Walmart know this and are entering the markets through the acquisition of businesses like Flipkart. With an existing base of online customers through Flipkart, Walmart hopes to take on Amazon and compete in the market.

Here are some statistics to keep in mind regarding what India's online ecosystem currently looks like.

The adjacent numbers can tell you a lot about how to take advantage of this large consumer base. In order to understand the market and its people, it's best to live in India or at least visit before undertaking a business venture. To be able to create and convert the consumers, you need to be able to see the challenges they face as well as the opportunities to disrupt with new technology.

The Indian consumer is a complex consumer. However, with more than 50% of the population under the age of 30, this is an opportunity to connect with younger, more digitally savvy consumers who are looking to improve their daily life experience.

INDIA'S DIGITAL OPPORTUNITY:

- Population: 1.38 billion
- Subscribers to telecom services: 1.1 billion
- Total internet users: 512 million
- Active social media users: 250 million
- E-commerce penetration: 26%
- M-commerce (mobile commerce) penetration: 20%
- M-wallet transactions: 3.02 billion (2017-2018)
- Mobile banking transactions: 1.87 billion (2017-2018)
- Number of digital buyers: 224 million (2018)

Sources: KPMG, Statisa, Hootsuite.

FINDING THE RIGHT PRICING

The right price in India is something that is seldom understood. You really will need to do your research specific to your field here, including checking competitor prices online and with various vendors, and be ready to allow for bargaining. With the advent of online stores and Amazon's aggressive growth, it's very easy to find and research competitors' pricing and to set your own price levels in accordance.

QUICK TIP

Demonetization allowed for mapping to now take place and for companies and the government to ultimately understand the users of various different states making it easier for those with products and services to offer smaller towns and cities the opportunity to market and engage. Please note these users also transact in their local language, which is not always English or Hindi, so if you are looking to offer something, look to enter the market via apps like 'PAYTM' which has a marketplace offering competitive pricing and its users are broad and more local in segments of the society. Smart villages are also a growing trend and one to watch.

INTELLECTUAL PROPERTY RISKS AND STRATEGIES

This is a quick guide to intellectual property risks and strategies.

As of 2018, India continues to be on the 'watchlist' for the protection and enforcement of intellectual property (IP). While there have been laws put in place to protect IP, the biggest issue in India has been the implementation of these laws.

The US government took initiatives with the Indian government to create local legislation to stop digital piracy. This initiative allows for '.in' domains that are infringing on information and content to be blocked or taken down if the owner of the domain does not verify or update content.

Other industry IP laws include:

- pharmaceutical and agrochemical products which can be patented in India
- the Design Law – while trade secrets are not protected in India, the Design Law was created to protect the counterfeit of designs and calls for the immediate destruction of counterfeits.

Quick guide to IP:

- Your trademarks and copyrights from home do not apply.
- Trade secrets are not protected.
- Designs must be submitted with limited protection of exact duplicates. Remember, someone can create a similar product with variations. This is one of the reasons many companies don't release new designs in India, but enter the market with older models that have less risk of duplication.
- You must apply for patents, trademarks and copyrights in the local market.
- The cost for applying for patents and trademarks in India is relatively low in comparison with the US and Europe. So, do it as soon as possible or someone else might!

STRATEGY
TO PROTECT
YOUR IDEAS

- Do find an attorney focused on corporate law to help you apply. The Indian government currently has programmes/schemes that can help you apply for patents at little to no cost.
- Don't share your idea if you know it's a market disruptor until you have submitted an application.
- Do have non-disclosure agreements signed specific to the local market.
- Design companies, beauty brands and manufacturers – enter the market with models and designs you can risk without having to show or give away your trade secrets.
- India is a complicated market when it comes to ideation and respect, so take the initiative to either not enter the market until you have built a strong brand or

enter with a strategic plan, so you
can weather the storm and see beyond
those who have duplicated your concept
or design.

It will get easier and laws will protect you, but make sure
that you are taking all legal steps in the beginning to protect your ideas, designs and concepts. Don't let this stop
you as this is a fact of business: competitors will always
look to make an existing product better.

CORRUPTION
AWARENESS AND
THE BRIBERY
ACT OF 2010

First, we want to share that India is slowly becoming a zero-tolerance country for bribes. As a country of over 1.3 billion people, corruption is something that isn't avoidable, but the government has been passing laws to reduce it.

Here are some acts and initiatives to bring about awareness and reduce corruption:

- Prevention Corruption Act (PC Act of 1988)
- Indian Penal Code IPC of 1960
- Central Vigilance Act of 2003
- Prevention of Money Laundering Act of 2002
- Right of Information Act of 2005
- The Bribery Act of 2010

These acts cover mail fraud and bribery to public officials or employees of companies in order to gain advantage over competitors. While we will not be going into detail here regarding bribes and corruption, we do want you to be aware that it may be tempting to take a shortcut, but it certainly is not a good idea. India is not the place to be to break the law as an expatriate. Most embassies take a neutral stance and allow the offenders to face criminal charges.

These acts have been initiatives by the different parties in power to help reduce corruption. For individuals from the UK, it's important to note that The Bribery Act of 2010 allows for legal action to be taken in the UK and holds you liable, with possible jail time.

The Bribery Act 2010 includes offenses such as:[1]

- Direct bribes to any official or person of interest in business, which is considered an 'active bribe'.
- Receiving a bribe, considered a 'passive bribe'.
- Directly trying to bribe a public official.
- Failure as a company to educate employees to avoid bribery.

Penalties range from imprisonment of ten years, termination of employment, being removed from bid lists, a media backlash, to being blacklisted and not being allowed to enter the country.

PART 10

BUSINESS BY REGION

DOING BUSINESS IN EAST INDIA

The eastern part of India, particularly cities like Kolkata (West Bengal) and Bhubaneswar (Odisha), has a long history of entrepreneurship from the colonial era. In fact, during much of its history, Kolkata was India's industrial engine. However, West Bengal faced a long period of stagnation under a Communist regime which was only ousted in 2012. With the formation of a new government in Bengal and the rise of business-friendly leaders in states like Odisha, eastern India now has good potential for entrepreneurs and investors.

The following are things for entrepreneurs to keep in mind if they look to do business in East India:

- West Bengal has a rich history of education and learning. The talent available in Kolkata is often highly educated and elite, owing to the good quality education provided at Calcutta University.

- Due to the stagnation during the Communist rule, people who studied in public schools in Bengal missed out on learning English. Hence, compared with other parts of India, people there might have less fluency in English. This is not true, however, for more elite parts of the workforce who have completed private schooling.
- According to consultants, Kolkata and Bengal suffer from a perception gap which prevents investors and entrepreneurs from coming to the state. However, the current government is trying to attract companies and capital to Bengal, positioning it as a growing IT hub.
- Accordingly, the Bengal Business summit was organized in February 2019, which focused on the strengths of Bengal as a place for investment.
- West Bengal, with a state GDP of $155.32 billion, is the fourth-largest contributor to India's services GDP and the sixth-largest contributor to manufacturing. It also has a consumer base of over 91 million people and serves as a strategic location gateway to Southeast Asia.
- Compared with other cosmopolitan cities like Delhi and Mumbai, costs of living and

operating a business are lower in Kolkata and Bhubaneswar, which can attract an early stage entrepreneur.

- Since many apps and services available in other big cities haven't spread as quickly to Kolkata and Bhubaneswar, there is a lot of opportunity for entrepreneurs who want to build similar networks within these states.

- Odisha is already a business-friendly state. It is India's mineral hub and enjoys industry-ready infrastructure. For example, it is ranked amongst the top four places for investment within India and has the fastest investment implementation rate in the whole country. The business-friendly government of Odisha has made it easy for entrepreneurs to assess the place for your business through the website Invest Odisha.

- Currently, Odisha's service industry contributes 51% to state GDP. Restaurants, financial and insurance services, transport, storage, communication and manufacturing are the leading industries in the state.

- For entrepreneurs planning to work in these states, remember that they are well-connected to the rest of India as well as Southeast Asia.

DOING BUSINESS IN NORTHEAST INDIA

There are eight regional provinces in Northeast India: Assam, Meghalaya, Nagaland, Arunachal Pradesh, Manipur, Sikkim, Mizoram and Tripura. Surrounded by Himalaya ranges, these states are rich in natural resources. However, tough geographical and climatic conditions have made them relatively isolated and inaccessible for the past few decades. However, in recent years, quick advances in infrastructure and technology have improved the integration of Northeast India. As per the 2011 census, Northeast India has a population of about 40 million and it also enjoys a high quality of human resources. Since this part of India has traditionally had relatively little investment, it can be immensely profitable for entrepreneurs.

According to the Indian Chamber of Commerce, Northeast India has potential for investment in agro-based industries, including tea production. Northeast India is also the source of the famous Assam and Darjeeling teas. There is also a growing interest in bamboo-based industries, medicinal and aromatic plants and sericulture.

Other investors and entrepreneurs might be attracted to the rich natural gas and mineral resources in these states.

Here are some things to keep in mind if you are an entrepreneur looking to work or invest in Northeast India:

- The biggest cities are Guwahati (Assam), Agartala (Tripura) and Dimapur (Nagaland).
- One can get scared off by reports of insurgency activity in Northeast India. However, keep in mind that not all states here suffer from this. For example, Sikkim is one of India's most peaceful states with a rich tradition of Buddhism. It is also India's only fully organic state focusing on organic farming and natural harvesting of crops, and has a high level of human development. Meghalaya, Mizoram and Tripura are also largely peaceful regions.
- Northeast India is culturally distinct from the rest of the nation with more than 200 ethnic groups forming the core of the community. Culturally, this part of India is also more matriarchal, and the influence of missionary education has led to a strong Christian community.

- Despite its relative isolation, Northeast India has a growing skilled workforce with English speaking abilities. Some of the well-known universities in this region are Northeastern Hill University (NEHU), the Indian Institute of Technology Guwahati, Sikkim Manipal University and Indian Institute of Management Shillong.
- The closest metropolitan city to Northeast India is the eastern city of Kolkata. If you need to set up a base near the Northeast, well-connected Kolkata is a good choice as the city is also an emerging IT hub.
- India is actively seeking more investment in the northeast as a means to enhance the development of the region. The 2018 Northeast India Development Scheme encourages micro-, small- and medium-scale enterprises to set up in this region. Under this scheme, the government has a huge range of incentives to attract investors and entrepreneurs. This includes reimbursement of GST and other federal level taxes, transport incentives and interest subsidies on capital credit. For more details, please see the Northeast India Development Scheme of 2018.

- Due to Northeast India's proximity to China, Myanmar and Bangladesh, it can also be a good launchpad for expanding into those markets.
- The human talent available in this region is adept at creative and service industries and people from the northeast are found in these professions all across India.

DOING
BUSINESS IN
WEST INDIA

Western areas, specifically Maharashtra and Gujarat, are at the centre of entrepreneurial India. Entrepreneurs looking to build a business in India should definitely consider these states. While these areas have typically been popular with big industries, they also offer a lot of opportunities to emerging entrepreneurs. With a large middle class, both these states offer a significant market. They also offer talented workers as they attract highly educated young people from across India.

Here are a few things to keep in mind if you are considering expanding your business in western India:

- Gujarat's economic miracle has been the subject of case studies in policy management classes. For example, the National Council of Applied Economic Research's State Investment Potential Index in both 2016 and 2017 ranked Gujarat as the topmost state. With 182 industrial complexes, eight Special Investment Regions and 21 Special Economic Zones, Gujarat is consistently ranked in the top four states in the World Bank's Ease of Doing Business in India.

- The entrepreneurial potential of Gujarat is likely to keep growing as 38% of the Delhi Mumbai Industrial Corridor lies in this state. Moreover, with the building of the Gujarat International Finance Tec-City (GIFT City) in Ahmedabad, the state is positioned as a hub of the International Financial Services Centre (IFSC) that caters to clients outside the jurisdiction of the domestic economy.

- In terms of demographics, Gujarat has a lot of advantages. Almost 70% of the population is under 55. Gujarat's population has also benefited from strong local governance for several decades and ranks highly in indices like education and human development. Ahmedabad, for example, is a hub of education, with institutes like the Indian Institute of Management Ahmedabad (the nation's top business school), the National Institute of Design (India's premier design school) and the Mudra Institute of Communication (the country's leading communications school). Hence, the city and the state provide a constant flow of some of India's brightest young people.

- For the past decade, Gujarat has each year hosted a summit for entrepreneurs. For any entrepreneur looking to expand into Gujarat or West India, this summit is an excellent start. Over the past four years, Gujarat has seen investment of $50 billion through this summit.

- Gujarat is also a leader in various sectors including petrochemicals, dairy, textiles, pharmaceuticals, automobiles, and gems and jewellery, amongst others.

- Maharashtra, with cities like Pune and Mumbai, is also a leading state for entrepreneurs in India. It is also consistently ranked amongst the top three states for investment in the nation and is regarded as the leading state for investors. Mumbai is the financial capital of India and is well-connected with the rest of the world.

- Leading cities in Maharashtra such as Mumbai and Pune attract talent from all over India. Mumbai draws talent from various parts of the world and is a rich source for quality human resources. It is the state with the highest GDP in India, the highest foreign direct investment and is home to many major corporate headquarters.

- Around 68% of Maharashtra's population is aged between 16 and 59. It also has several high-quality public and private universities which make it easy to hire good talent.
- Maharashtra has industrial clusters in sectors such as automotive, IT and ITeS (information technology enabled services), chemicals, textiles and food processing, and offers investment opportunities in these sectors.
- The world's largest film industry in terms of viewership, Bollywood, is based out of Mumbai. For entrepreneurs who want to work in creative sectors, this is a logical place to begin.

DOING BUSINESS IN NORTH INDIA

The northern part of India is home to some of India's fastest-growing cities in the areas of health and wellness, the food industry, beauty and technology markets. It is also the home of India's national capital (Delhi), India's first airport city 'Aerocity' and the fourth busiest airport in the world.

From Delhi to Rajasthan, north India, although land-locked, holds many opportunities for global entrepreneurs and foreign investors. With a dynamic pool of potential employees who are fluent in English, it's a good entry point. These cities host expatriate communities and their citizens are often familiar with dealing with foreigners. If you are looking to do business with government and strategic partnerships, Delhi is the place to be.

Here are a few things to keep in mind if you are considering expanding your business in north India:

DELHI

Delhi is home to the leaders of India: the prime minister, president, Lok Sabha (the lower house of Parliament) and the main state government. If you want to do business with the government of India, Delhi is where you need to be.

HARYANA

With its main district being Gurugram (Gurgaon), the state of Haryana is home to a vast number of tech start-ups with government incentive programmes to attract new companies and offer them tax incentives and access to schemes that will help them maximize earnings and promote job growth. Home of Tier 2 and 3 cities (see chart) such as Faridabad, Panipat and Ambala, the state continues to focus on infrastructure and providing its citizens with accessibility to quality transportation and lifestyle improvements. In order to achieve this, it offers incentives to hotel and manufacturing companies to grow within the state.

TIER 1 AND TIER 2 CITIES IN INDIA

States/UTs	Cities Classified as Tier I	Cities Classified as Tier II
Andhra Pradesh	Hyderabad	Vijayawada, Warangal, Vishapatnam, Guntur
Assam		Guwahati
Bihar		Patna
Chandigarh		Chandigarh
Chhattisgarh		Durg-Bhilai, Raipur
Delhi	Delhi	
Gujarat		Ahmedabad, Rajkot, Jamnagar, Vadodara, Surat
Haryana		Faridabad
Jammu and Kashmir		Srinagar, Jammu
Jharkhand		Jamshedpur, Dhanbad, Ranchi
Karnataka	Bengaluru	Belgaum, Hubli-Dhanbad, Mangalore, Mysore
Kerala		Kozhikode, Kochi, Thiruvanathpuram
Madhya Pradesh		Gwalior, Indore, Bhopal, Jabalpur
Maharashtra	Mumbai	Amravati, Nagpur, Aurangabad, Nashik, Bhiwandi, Pune, Solapur, Kolhapur
Orissa		Cuttack, Bhubaneswar
Punjab		Amritsar, Jalandhar, Ludhina
Pondicherry		Pondicherry
Rajasthan		Bikaner, Jaipur, Jodhpur, Kota
Tamil Nadu	Chennai	Salem, Tiruppur, Coimbatore, Tiruchirappalli, Madurai
Uttar Pradesh		Moradabad, Meerut, Ghaziabad, Aligarh, Agra, Bareilly, Lucknow, Kanpur, Allahabad, Gorakhpur, Varanasi
Uttarakhand		Dehradun
West Bengal	Kolkata	Asansol

*Reference https://www.mapsofindia.com/maps/India/tier-1-and-2-cities.html

TIER 3 CITIES
IN INDIA

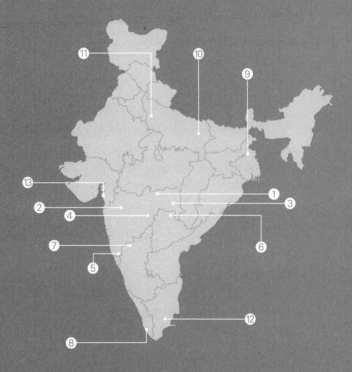

1   Amravati (Maharashtra)
2   Aurangabad (Maharashtra)
3   Chandrapur (Maharashtra)
4   Nanded (Maharashtra)
5   Belgam (Karnataka)

6   Adilabad (Telangana)
7   Bijapur (Karnataka)
8   Ernakulam (Kerala)
9   Murshidabad (West Bengal)
10 Varanasi (UP)

11 Agra (UP)
12 Madurai (Tamil Nadu)
13 Surat (Gujrat)

Reference Tier 3 Cities:
https://www.quora.com/What-are-tier-3-cities-What-are-some-examples-of-tier-3-cities-in-India

HIMACHAL PRADESH

Himachal Pradesh is home to cities such as Shimla, its capital Manali and Dharamshala, the home of the Dalai Lama. Himachal Pradesh also neighbours China and Tibet, making it attractive to those looking to explore the Himalayas. It also hosts an array of farms, focusing on organic and natural harvesting of crops such as vegetables, flowers, fruits and minerals such as copper, rock salt, mica and natural gas. Himachal Pradesh is a must for those looking to understand more about India's health and wellness ecosystem. A slew of new natural wellness food brands are emerging from the region, with specializations in honey and cheese.

JAMMU KASHMIR

Jammu Kashmir is most often in the news due to its proximity to Pakistan, but it is also home to some of the most expensive mushrooms. The Guchchi mushroom, once thought of as most expensive than gold, grows in the foothills of the Himalayas and can range from $180-$500 per kilogram. Other exotic ingredients from the region include Kashmir saffron and Quality Darjeeling tea which is often sought out by tea connoisseurs. Although the area has suffered due to the border tensions, it is an excellent location for those looking to enter the local goods and leather markets.

PUNJAB

We often hear of Punjabi food, music, DJs and dance, but Punjab also offers an array of opportunities for entrepreneurs. The local leaders host and promote local investment and have made an effort to reduce the difficulty of doing business in the region. With Tier 2 cities such as Chandigarh, the state of Punjab hosts skilled workers in both the arts and technology with some of the largest numbers of tech graduates. There is a great opportunity here for foreign companies to hire some of the best talent.

CHANDIGARH

The Tier 2 city of the state of Punjab, Chandigarh is a union territory known for being part of the smart cities programme. It also has been renowned as one of the best cities in India in terms of ease of living and doing business. The city, designed by Swiss-French modernist architect Le Corbusier, is ahead of its time with a unique look and feel. Today Chandigarh is home to an international airport, a city with new digital infrastructure and is known to be safe for foreigners.

RAJASTHAN

The land where the kings once lived is now home to many remaining beautiful palaces. The city of Jaipur has some of the best educational institutions in the country and is becoming an education hub in the north, with a diverse pool of talented graduates in technology but also in specialized arts such as Indian embroidery. Rajasthan also offers beautiful desserts. For entrepreneurs in fashion retail and art, Rajasthan can open your eyes and allow you to find artisans to partner with who can give you a global edge. Rajasthan is home to scenic states, including Jodhpur, Udaipur and Jaisalmer.

CITIES TO DO BUSINESS IN ALONG THE TAJ EXPRESS HIGHWAY

From Delhi to Kannauj, this section provides a quick look at age-old industries that have potential for local and global growth. There are great opportunities in these industries for entrepreneurs exploring the consumer goods segments. By focusing on doing business and researching cities within a few hours of Delhi, you can maximize your networks and understand more about the potential opportunities in the north of India.

Three cities that have growth potential in the aromatherapy, perfume, glass and pottery industries are: Kannauj India, Firozabad and Khurja.

KANNAUJ INDIA
'THE LAND OF PERFUMES'

Kannauj is located 440km from Delhi, known as the perfume capital of India and the 'Grasse of the East'. Kannauj Perfume has been registered and protected through the agreement on Trade-Related Aspects of Intellectual Property Rights (TRIPS) agreement. Kannauj is a hidden gem for those in the development of food manufacturing and consumer goods and looking to locally source ingredients and retain traditional distillation techniques unique only to the city and residents who have learned and passed them down through the generations.

For centuries the city of Kannauj has been the home to an old distillation method that involves clay and steam distilleries. The technique has been handed down for hundreds of years to members of the family. The roses of Kannauj are one of the most popular due to farmers delivering the petals to local distilleries (700 to 150 in the past decade) where traditional methods take place to extract the oils.

'Attar', meaning 'fragrant oil', is used in various formulas and can be very expensive due to the complex distillation process that incorporates clay pots and original, outdated hardware to maintain the consistency of the original attar which is often incorporated in perfume formulations.

For entrepreneurs looking to explore Kannauj, you have an opportunity to learn about a 500-year-old distillation process only taught in the town of Kanauji. But, more importantly, the essential oil industry for beauty and aromatherapy products is growing. Indian consumers want natural and less synthetic formulas.

As nearly 3,000 people in Kanauji engage in the attar industry directly or indirectly, the government of India created the Fragrance and Flavour Development Corporation (FFDC) Kannauj to create strategic partnerships and promote the growth of the region to open up to foreign investors as well as brands who are looking to explore and promote growth in the area.

To learn more about Kannauj, its history and industry potential, visit the FFDC website and, if possible, travel to the city. The FFDC holds various different workshops throughout the year, and it is an excellent opportunity to enroll on one of these workshops to further understand the process of aromatherapy.

FIROZABAD
'THE GLASS CAPITAL'

If you have ever dreamed about owning your own glass design company, Firozabad is the place to explore. Firozabad, approximately 200km away from the capital city of Delhi, has a lot to offer those who are into the creative art of design and interested in exploring India's glass bangles industry. Known as the glass bangle capital of the world, it offers the creative entrepreneur a place to explore the art of glassblowing in its more primitive state.

Firozabad is the perfect place to explore glass packaging options, as well as designing and creating drinking glasses that are unique to your brand. The art of glass-making bangles has been established here for over 200 years, and while there are hundreds of factories in the area, many practise the art right in their homes. Glass bangles are incredibly culturally important. Indian women often showcase a collection of bangles during wedding ceremonies to signify a newly married bride.

KHURJA
'THE LAND OF POTTERY'

When you visit most five-star hotels you will often find exquisite plates and mugs. If you turn them over, you will notice that 80% of Indian crockery comes from Khurja. Khurja is host to a 500-year-old pottery technique considered the most traditional of Indian pottery. Unlike Firobad, Khurja is home to many colleges and host to art fairs. The city is also easily accessible via the Delhi to Calcutta line. If you love the art of plating and plates and want to make a mark on kitchen and lifestyle design, this is a great start.

Khurja is about a two-hour drive from the city of Delhi and is home to over 25,000 workers in the pottery/

ceramics industry. The process of making the pottery is one that has been passed down through generations, but it can be learned by foreigners as well. The process of Khurja pottery and ceramic is one that can be lengthy and tiring, involving clay, moding and glazing each item by hand.

The demand for these products is continuing to grow both locally and globally, especially as local consumers improve their standard of living. The government of India is aggressively seeking growth opportunities for this region and its citizens, so do a little homework and you may find yourself in the next big trend or partnering with the supplier and manufacturer.

Here are a few things to keep in mind if you are considering expanding your business in north India:

- North India is home to major Tier 1, 2 and 3 cities.
- It has over 30% of India's population.
- It is also the home of three of India's 'unicorns' – OYO, Snapdeal and Paytm, all of which have corporate offices in the Delhi region.
- It's the home of the first airport city 'Aerocity'.
- There are many online expatriate groups to join to start building relationships.

- PHD Chamber of Commerce offers a variety of schemes and can help connect foreign investors and entrepreneurs to local programmes specifically in Delhi.
- Rajasthan holds special programmes for Korean and Japanese investors/entrepreneurs.
- Punjab University is open to inviting guest speakers to the region to interact with students and local business owners. It is also the hub of the startup cell in Chandigarh.
- Honda and many other car manufacturers have turned to the talent and skills on offer in Punjab. The Make India initiative has been integral for the Punjab region.

If you are going to do business in north India, remember that you're dealing with an intelligent consumer base and one of India's higher income populations. Also remember that what works in places like Chandigarh may not work in Delhi. One of the most challenging yet interesting things about doing business in India is that its consumer population is as diverse as its workforce. Consumers are always looking for deals, but the younger generation is keen to build more mature, educated and committed relationships with brands than previous generations.

DOING BUSINESS IN SOUTH INDIA

South India is one of the more advanced areas of India for technology growth as the tech boom of outsourcing had its early beginnings here and it remains the hub for the IT industry. South India is also home to many temples and is a more predominantly conservative and traditional part of the country.

Here are a few things to keep in mind if you are considering expanding your business in South India:[1]

- States in South India include: Karnataka, Kerala, Telangana (Hyderabad), Tamil Nadu (Chennai) and Andhra Pradesh (Bangalore). Places such as Pondicherry and the Andaman and Nicobar Islands are found here.
- The population totals about 290 million.
- The state of Telangana hosted the Global Entrepreneurship Summit 2017, giving it global exposure.

- The south is a major hub for manufacturing, healthcare, automotive, IT and fintech companies. It's also a hub for textile mills in cities such as Coimbatore and Madurai.
- Bangalore remains a major tech hub for the country with companies such as Wipro and Infosys, and is often referred to as 'India's Silicon Valley'. There is also a huge presence of pharmaceutical companies with labs and research and development centres in the city.
- Major business sectors in Kerala include construction, shipbuilding, transportation, shipping, seafood and spices, chemical industries, IT, tourism, health services and banking. Kochi (Cochin) is widely referred to as the commercial capital of Kerala. In recent years the city has witnessed heavy investment, thus making it one of the fastest-growing Tier 2 cities in India. Thiruvananthapuram (Trivandrum) is the state capital.
- Because of its diversity, South India is home to many different languages as each region has its own language. These include Tamil, Telugu, Carnatic and Mariati.

PART 11

CONCLUSION: THE EVER-CHANGING DEVELOPMENT OF INDIA

As a developing country, India continues to be ever-changing. Every part of this extraordinary country is evolving as new ideas, modern shifts and economic growth continues. Barriers that existed in India even a generation ago are being broken down, aspirations and achievements once thought unthinkable are being reached and doors are being opened by economic reform, globalization, technology advancement, ambitious visionaries and a mindset shift in ancient cultural practices.

This book is intended as a general introduction to India's diverse and complex culture and its business practices; it is in no way definitive or all-inclusive, as each enterprise and entrepreneur brings their own individual needs and character. Keep in mind, there is little that can be labeled simply as 'Indian' culture. Each region, business sector and culture will have its own nuances that make it impossible to have a uniform approach to understanding the full scope of India's social or business culture. The information and guidance in this book are meant for encouraging international business relationships while understanding the metacultural commonalities. With these valuable insights, mutually enriching and prosperous business partnerships can flourish.

As two female entrepreneurs, we would like other female entrepreneurs to know and understand that India has a lot to offer you. A revolution of female entrepreneurs in India is changing the landscape by creating platforms in education, technology, women's only social network's, health and wellness, travel, media, management and more while leading with vision and strength. India's government is investing in its female population by making it easier for them to enter the workforce, as well as encouraging innovation and an increase in STEM programmes to harness their creative energy.

In India, there is great potential to collaborate between regions and facilitate local growth. A recent survey found that many Indians are still fearful of failure when starting their own businesses, and while many see that there are opportunities available, they are not yet jumping fast enough.[1] By starting up a business in India, you can act as a mentor and coach to inspire new entrepreneurs and those who might need a boost of guidance and encouragement.

We hope this book has inspired those who have considered doing business in India to spark action in moving forward to create business partnerships along with an appreciation for this extraordinary country. While you may face some challenges in setting up your business abroad, remember that they are just temporary as you work together in achieving a common goal. By visiting and exploring India and its government resources available for businesses, you could be the one launching the next 'unicorn' in a country with more than a billion potential consumers.

Doing business in India may seem overwhelming or difficult but we want to assure you that once you navigate through the cultural business behaviours and expectations, doing business with Indians can be an extremely rewarding, enriching and prosperous experience. When Indians and foreigners learn to understand each other and work together, new ideas and potential begin to unfold. There are many qualities that make Indians a pleasure to work with, while others will leave you scratching your head. Indians have strong work ethics, are eager to learn, and are respectful, loyal and easy going. At the end of the day Indians want what most of us want; to care for our families, prepare the next generation for a better future and to leave a legacy of success – together we can achieve all of this in incredible India.

BIBLIOGRAPHY

WHY DOING BUSINESS IN INDIA IS A GOOD IDEA

1 "India's GDP expected to grow at 7.3% in 2018-19", The Economic Times, 9 January, 2019
https://economictimes.indiatimes.com/news/economy/indicators/indias-gdp-expected-to-grow-at-7-3-in-2018-19/articleshow/67451511.cms

2 "The World's Top 20 Economies", Investopedia, 22 May, 2019
https://www.investopedia.com/insights/worlds-top-economies

3 "Top 5 Increasingly Booming Industries in India", Silicon India News, 26 December, 2018
https://www.siliconindia.com/news/general/Top-5-Increasingly-Booming-Industries-in-India-nid-206416-cid-1.html

4 "All of the top 10 fastest growing cities in the world are in India", World Economic Forum, 19 December, 2018
https://www.weforum.org/agenda/2018/12/all-of-the-world-s-top-10-cities-with-the-fastest-growing-economies-will-be-in-india/

5 "India Population Live", World o Meters, 25 May, 2019
http://www.worldometers.info/world-population/india-population/

6 "Richest Cities of India", Business World, 26 May, 2019
http://www.businessworld.in/article/Richest-Cities-Of-India/28-06-2017-121011/

7 "Economic Activity", Office of the Registrar General & Census Commissioner, India,
http://censusindia.gov.in/Census_And_You/economic_activity.aspx

POPULATION

1 "Population of Cities in India", World Population Review, 2019
http://worldpopulationreview.com/countries/india-population/cities/

2 "India Population 2019", World Population Review, May, 2019
http://worldpopulationreview.com/countries/india-population/

GOVERNMENT AND POLITICS

1 Start Up India Website: Global Partnerships – Korea, Japan India Relations
https://www.startupindia.gov.in/content/sih/en/international.html

WELL- KNOWN INDIANS

1 "Isha Ambani", The Famous People
https://www.thefamouspeople.com/profiles/isha-ambani-33705.php

2 "Salman Khan tops Forbes India Celebrity 100 list for third time in a row", Forbes India, 5 December, 2018,
http://www.forbesindia.com/article/2018-celebrity-100/salman-khan-tops-forbes-india-celebrity-100-list-for-third-time-in-a-row/51955/1

ART, MUSIC, DANCE, BOLLYWOOD

1 "Why Aamir Khan Is Arguably The World's Biggest Movie Star", Forbes, 5 October, 2017
https://www.forbes.com/sites/robcain/2017/10/05/heres-why-aamir-khan-is-arguably-the-worlds-biggest-movie-star-part-2/#65ba12218444

STEREOTYPES AND MISCONCEPTIONS

1 "10% quota to be implemented in 40,000 colleges, about 900 universities in India", India Today, 15 January, 2019
https://www.indiatoday.in/education-today/news/story/10-quota-law-prakash-javadekar-10-percent-reservation-divd-1431209-2019-01-15

2 "STATS ABOUT LITERACY IN INDIA: NATIONAL EDUCATION DAY 2018", Seruds India, 9 November, 2018
https://www.serudsindia.org/stats-about-literacy-in-india-2018/

3 "India's billionaires: A swelling tribe", Forbes India, 6 April, 2017
http://www.forbesindia.com/article/special/indias-billionaires-a-swelling-tribe/46581/1

4 "Countries With The Highest Rates Of Vegetarianism", World Atlas, 1 May, 2017
https://www.worldatlas.com/articles/countries-with-the-highest-rates-of-vegetarianism.html

5 "Vegetarianism by Country", Maria Online, 25 May, 2019
https://www.maria-online.us/travel/article.php?lg=en&q=Vegetarianism_by_country

TRAVEL, HEALTH AND SAFETY

1 "World's top airports for Customer Experience revealed", Airports Council International, 6 March, 2019
https://aci.aero/news/2019/03/06/worlds-top-airports-for-customer-experience-revealed/

TOP TRAVEL DESTINATIONS AND ATTRACTIONS

1 "10 million foreign tourists visited India last year; $27 B earned from the tourism sector", Think Change India, 23 January, 2018
https://yourstory.com/2018/01/foreign-tourists-india-tourism-sector

2 "India to be 3rd largest tourism economy in 10 years", Times of India, 23 March, 2018
https://m.timesofindia.com/india/report-india-to-be-3rd-largest-tourism-economy-in-10-years/amp_articleshow/63421777.cms

3 "WTTC predicts a massive growth of India's tourism economy", Tourism India, September, 2018
http://www.tourismindiaonline.com/detail/index.php?cnws=368&crnpg=headlines

4 "Tourism In Kerala", Kerala Culture
http://www.keralacultural.com/kerala-tourism.html

MARKET OPPORTUNITIES

1 "8.2 Million jobs needed annually in India to keep employment rates constant", Live Mint, 17 April, 2018
https://www.livemint.com/Politics/Zo7TysdEEqp4PdDv7rV8BK/News-in-Numbers-82-million-jobs-needed-annually-in-India-t.html

2 "India Election 2019: A Simple Guide to the World's Largest Vote",
   The New York Times, 22 May, 2019
   https://www.nytimes.com/interactive/2019/world/asia/india-election.html

BUSINESS WISDOM
1 "India Preparing For The Biggest Migration On The Planet", Invest India Blog,
   2 January, 2018
   https://www.investindia.gov.in/team-india-blogs/
   india-preparing-biggest-human-migration-planet

LEGAL AND REGULATORY FRAMEWORK
1 FDI Policy, Invest India Website
   https://www.investindia.gov.in/foreign-direct-investment

FDI RESTRICTIONS TO CONSIDER
1 Foreign Direct Investment Policy in India
   https://www.investindia.gov.in/foreign-direct-investment

2 Press Release, Ministry of Commerce and Industry, FDI Policy on e-commerce
   http://pib.nic.in/PressReleaseIframePage.aspx?PRID=1562493

TAXATION AND GOVERNMENT INCENTIVES
1 Taxation in India, Invest India Website
   https://www.investindia.gov.in/taxation

CORRUPTION AWARENESS AND THE BRIBERY ACT OF 2010
1 "Welcome Changes to Anti-Corruption Law", The Hindu Business Line, 15 August, 2018
   https://www.thehindubusinessline.com/opinion/columns/welcome-changes-to-anti-
   corruption-law/article24697638.ece

DOING BUSINESS IN SOUTH INDIA
1 Invest India Website
   https://www.investindia.gov.in/

CONCLUSION: THE EVER-CHANGING DEVELOPMENT OF INDIA
1. Shukla, S., Parray, M.I., Chatwal, N.S., Bharti, P. & Dwivedi, A.K. (2019),
   "GEM India Report – 2017/18". Emerald Publishing India New-Delhi.
   (ISBN: 9781786354235)

ABOUT THE AUTHORS

JAMIE CID is a social entrepreneur and consultant focusing on digital branding, strategic partnerships and international relations. She travels between Delhi and NY as a motivational speaker and is the founder of MobiHires (mobihires.com), a next-generation job app. Jamie is called on by NGOs, companies and senior executives to come up with creative solutions to strengthen their global positioning. She helps companies launch new products, and she was the lead in a project funded by Google to launch the first crowdsourcing human rights platform (movements.org) connecting activists and journalists around the world. Her career started on Wall Street and progressed into entrepreneurship when she launched her first company – a skin-care line called SAIJADE.

To collaborate with Jamie and her team of experts on launching and doing business in India contact her via email at **jamie@mobihires.com** or follow her on Twitter **@jamiecid**.

LAURIE BAUM often calls India home, where she's held positions as International Executive Director: ALL Ladies League, Global Ambassador: Women Economic Forum, International Programs Director: Rising Star Outreach, Director of Special Events: Days for Girls International and as a Professor of English Communication and Life Skills: Rai University, Ahmedabad. Laurie's role in these organizations has helped foster economic progression, social entrepreneurship, women's empowerment and youth leadership skills. Laurie is an Indian business culture consultant, offering training to help minimize cross-cultural mishaps and misunderstandings. She is also a channel partner facilitator and international communications advisor. When Laurie is not in India, she can be found exploring other parts of the world. Laurie is always drawn back to the US where her family provides a loving and joyful place to land.

To book Laurie for Indian business collaboration, speaking engagements or travel tours to India, visit **www.starrylaurie.com**.